MW01506204

THE
Season

Other books by Tom Kelly:

Tenth Legion

T.H. Kelly Handbook

Dealer's Choice

Better on a Rising Tide

The Boat

A Year Outside

Faces in the Crowd

A Few Loose Chapters

Take Back in Fancy

Hat Full of Rabbits

A Fork in the Road

'Ol Tom and Laura

Absent Companions

Infirm Opinions

Payback

Their Old Inhabitants

Point of View

Matter of Context

The Other Seven

No Place to Hide

Around the Edges

Unfaded Roses

With a Little Bit of Luck

Infinite Variety

THE
Season

TOM KELLY

www.tomkellyinc.com

CONTENTS

1

ANTICIPATION

The last active element of the Confederate Army was a unit that never fought, but only paraded, and had, in addition to its lack of combat time, several other peculiarities. It was composed of only two soldiers, one of whom was nearly ninety and the other just under five. The muster rolls of the Confederate Army have no record of its existence, as if it were a secret force. And, strangest of all, it did not march under the Stars and Bars but marched under the flag of the United States, a circumstance neither of its members seemed to find the least bit out of the ordinary.

If its table of organization was unusual, its table of equipment was even sketchier. Neither of its members was uniformed, one of them frequently paraded barefoot, and, in addition to the wrong flag, its only other equipment was a drum and a sword.

The drum was not even a real drum. It was one of those

tin cake boxes that held Smith Bakery's Christmas fruitcakes. After the first Christmas, this musical field expedient was replaced with a real drum, courtesy of Santa Claus. Supply in the Confederate Army had a tendency to be both late and spotty and sometimes come from unusual sources. On the other hand, the sword was authentic from the beginning. Not only was it authentic, it was bright. Crack regiments in this army were sometimes shoeless, but the weapons were invariably operable.

Uncle Johnny, by virtue of his white hair and mustaches, carried the flag and marched in front. My place was to beat the drum and march behind, wearing the sword. More dragging it than wearing it, actually, since it was a regulation cavalry saber, had been made for a trooper older than age four, and the belt went completely around me twice and tended to slip down a lot. None of this bothered me. I understood even then that you fight with the weapons you are issued, and that only a poor workman blames failure on his tools.

I realize now that Uncle Johnny was simply enjoying the fantasies of a little boy. It was different with me. I was in dead earnest and as serious as a train wreck. I was deadly serious because there was a gap in my education: I did not know that the war had been over for more than sixty-five years.

I knew, of course, that we were not doing all that well. I had understood some of the conversations I had heard between Uncle Johnny and some of his friends, but I didn't let a lot of it concern me. Next year, when I got bigger, Uncle Johnny and I were going to help, and as soon as the first team got there, things were going to look up. I was confident of that because we had talked about it.

What we had not talked about was my private worry, the thing I kept secret: the fact that I couldn't button my pants to my shirt by myself.

Little boys in the 1930s wore short pants without belts.

ANTICIPATION

The pants buttoned in the fly. Zippers, if invented, had not yet penetrated to south Alabama. I could handle the fly, but the pants buttoned to the shirt with two big buttons in the front and two in the back, and the ones in the back were beyond me.

Hopefully, things were going to be noisy when we got to the war. There were bound to be artillery duels and cavalry charges, and a lot of the noise and smoke and yelling like I saw in the movies. Surely there would be a moment or two where I could privately slip over to Uncle Johnny and get him to button the back buttons quietly, where nobody could see us. It bothered me to have this flaw in my character, this inability to dress myself completely. But I did not consider it to be of critical importance.

Of course, I had never heard of the management principle of informed neglect — the one that says you overlook extraneous faults while addressing the big problem — but I applied it instinctively. We had to go. The boys needed help even if it came from people with improperly buttoned pants, and we would simply have to tend to these minor defects after we got there.

Until then, my understanding of anticipation had consisted of looking forward to good things that were going to happen on their own. The approach of Christmas, or my birthday, or a visit to my grandmother's and a slice of her mince pie. Attendance at this war was going to involve anticipation of an entirely different breed of cat altogether.

It was going to require me to do something personally, rather than sit still and let it happen. It was going to have a thorn or two among the roses. I was looking forward to it, all right; but somewhere around in the back, there were some faintly disturbing noises.

I am now a hell of a long way from four-and-a-half and have had almost all of those early, dim perceptions cleared up. I know now that anticipation, like a coin, has two sides, and one of them can be painful. In certain circumstances, there are species of anticipation that can best be defined as dread.

In certain other instances, anticipation can be pleasurable, but absolutely rigid and formal, like the entrance of the matadors into the bullring, or the infield and batting practice taken by both teams before the ball game.

Or, it can take the shape of the formalized ritual conducted in preparation for the spring turkey season: lengthy and subtle anticipation, multiple anticipation, compound anticipation in all of its complexities and colors.

This ritual always starts at the same time, in the second or third week of January, and in the same way. It starts with the appearance of the alder catkins.

Here along the Gulf Coast, we don't have enough winter to count, even though it did get to one degree below zero in Mobile on Mardi Gras Day of 1899 — which makes you wonder what the hell it was that morning in Bozeman, Montana — but if you move here from North Dakota you won't notice the winter at all, unless someone points it out to you. But we are not truly tropical, and the trees do go into dormancy, and break dormancy depending upon the amount of cold, relatively speaking. The year before last, for example, I saw red maple in the river swamp, in flower on Christmas Eve. But year after year, warm or cold, there are tag-alder catkins by the 20th of January.

An event perhaps not quite as spectacular as ice-out on the Yukon, but the earliest sign we have to offer.

Tag alder — *Ainus serrulata,* to get technical — is classified properly as a shrub, ranges from middle Florida to upper New England — where you can bet your sweet ass it don't have catkins by the 20th of January — and, as far as I can tell,

ANTICIPATION

has no commercial value whatsoever. But then, of course, neither does a rainbow.

An alder catkin, which is the male flower, is about 1/4 inch in diameter, 2 inches or so long, and as it ripens is loaded with the pollen, as fine as flour and as yellow as powdered sulfur. During the second week of January, pick off a branch to take home and show somebody that spring is really coming, and the backseat of the car will be covered with yellow dust when you get there.

Burt Spiller used to talk about alder a lot in his woodcock stories, but I didn't know we had it here in Alabama until I was grown. I always figured it was one of those exotic New England species, like sugar maple or tamarack. You can't eat it, or wear it, or make anything out of it, except maybe a switch to hit a kid with; but when you see it, you know the sun has been started back north for a good two weeks. Never mind what the thermometer says, it is the first thing that triggers your thought processes toward the upcoming spring season, which, in turn, leads you naturally to speculation on the state of the inventory.

Turkeys have certain characteristics that make them difficult to deal with, and one of these idiosyncrasies is the difficulty of inventory. They don't stay still long enough to let you count them accurately. They can easily be baited to observation points — a turkey probably baits easier than a duck — and they fall into the habit of coming to the bait at about the same time every day. A bait count cannot be called a true census, however, because there is no basis for estimating that portion of the population that did not visit the bait sites during the count.

There are schemes that can take a lot of the guesswork out of such a count, and there is no question but that, properly done and properly recorded, it gives a good idea of population changes and trends. Never good enough to satisfy people like auditors, who lie awake at night and worry about timber cruises that count stationary trees to +/- 10 percent, but good enough for amateurs.

There are two eminently suitable times for bait counts.

Turkey flocks are more stable and population movement is at a minimum during the six weeks after September 1st and the six weeks after January 15th. Turkeys also take grain baits better then, than at other times.

My own personal preference for a bait count is the period after the middle of January.

The only things open to hunting in February are snipe and quail, the weather is generally cold, the river bottoms are in flood, which tends to better concentrate the flocks on the uplands, and you are not looking over both shoulders for the next hurricane, a common occupation around here during September and the first half of October.

To get decent coverage, you must have a bait site for each 500 acres — they need to be no closer than two-thirds of a mile apart in all directions — and it takes a while to get things set up. You have to get birds coming to the bait sites and call in enough favors to get all the count sites manned on the day or days you make the tally. All this usually takes a couple of weeks, which has you making the count around the second week of February.

Count procedures ought to be standardized: the same baits, the same sites, the same dates used each year, to give commonality to the results, and it is considered desirable to make the count twice and take the higher of the two.

All in all, it is a good way to use up part of the anticipatorial season, it gives you a good idea of what you have to hunt, and, best of all, it yields reliable data to enable you to detect marked changes in the population, if there are any.

There are almost as many opinions about what constitutes good populations as there are about the speed of horses; but lately, experienced biologists tend to agree that one turkey per 25 acres is outstanding, and anything from there down to one turkey per 40 to 50 acres is considered good.

Turkeys are, at best, secretive, elusive, and hard to count. If you are trying to establish a dove field, you plant whatever it is you propose to use, harvest it in whatever way is considered legal, and, after the birds start using it, you can go there any afternoon and watch the flights come in over the trees to feed. My only trouble is that I don't know how to estimate the numbers after they get there. I hear people say with every sign of utter sincerity that such and such a field has 1,000 birds, or 1,500, or whatever, but I can't do this; and secretly, I am not all that sure there are a lot of people who can. Leaving concrete numbers aside, you see a lot of doves, you see them flying around the field most of the afternoon, and you are therefore able to schedule a shoot with a degree of confidence.

Nobody can lean on the same fence post on several successive afternoons and say he has a turkey per 40 acres. He can say it, of course, but he has no basis for the estimate.

One of these days, after I have gotten rich and powerful, I am going to arrange to have two dozen old gobblers trapped and fitted with transmitters. Then I will have a dozen of the oldest, wisest, most experienced hunters I know — people old and wise and skillful in my opinion, not necessarily in theirs — all fitted with transmitters. Next we will have a three-day hunt, turn everybody loose on the same 8,000 acres, and plot the whole thing with telemetry for the entire time.

The next week, after all the data has been recorded, assessed, and plotted, we are going to have a big dinner party, I will be the master of ceremonies, and will exhibit, in lieu of after-dinner speeches, how many of these direct lineal descendants of Daniel Boone were within 100 yards of a big turkey, because it shows so on the plot, and nobody saw a thing.

Nobody except the turkeys, of course, and they won't be at the dinner.

There are going to be red faces, and shifty eyes, and accusations of dirty dealings, and, in certain cases, a flat refusal to accept perfectly evident and provable scientific facts. (There is a specific word for that — I just can't think of it right now.)

Friendships are going to be strained, in some cases damaged irremediably, and tempers lost. But it will clearly make the point just how hard turkeys are to count, and just how easy it is to come to the conclusion that there ain't none left.

Every group that hunts together, whether it is a club on leased land, a group hunting public land, or a sole owner who hunts the ancestral acres and has friends who help him, will invariably have one of those three- or four-day periods when turkeys simply quit gobbling and the flag will be raised to announce: "We ought to do something — there ain't none left."

The adjoining club baited them all away, or the poachers or the varmints got them, or it is this damned clear-cutting that ran them off, or there has to be an outbreak of blackhead in the flock.

Clearly, there has to be some outside agency responsible, somebody has sinned, and by God we need to get the bottom of this and punish the guilty bastard!

You can't stop this kind of behavior. Paranoia has been with us always, but with a decent inventory, this brand of it can be reduced from outright mutiny to sullen muttering, and when the turkeys do start gobbling again, nobody has made so many outrageous statements that he has to eat crow or go into seclusion for the balance of the season.

During the spring season of 1968, hunting on a place that

ran one turkey per 25 acres and had maintained such a population since the early 1950s, I did not hear a single gobble from the 20th of March to the 25th of April.

We saw turkeys all year. They were seen in pastures. They were in green patches in the afternoon. You ran them off the roost on your way into the woods in the morning, and they crossed the road in front of the car when you were leaving to go home.

During the course of the season, a couple of them walked up to my yelping, lay down on the sacrificial altar, handed me the knife, and I obliged them; but from beginning to end, the season was conducted in silence.

The only turkey I heard gobble all year did it the first morning of the fall season: November 15th.

We had no inventory in those days, except the half-assed opinions of the club members, opinions normally formed by one tour through the road system when the annual meeting was held, on the first weekend of October.

Some of the comments on the silence defied belief.

One of the club members, an industrial psychologist by profession, whose head was packed with pseudo-scientific rubbish of the most virulent type, was firmly convinced it was some species of mass hypnosis, like those fiery crosses that were supposed to have appeared to Crusaders on their way to the Holy Land in 1250, or the ghostly appearance of the Grail, floating in midair, seen by everyone at Arthur's table.

Two or three of the most paranoid were convinced that the State had infiltrated a secret group of biologists with cannon traps, and they had trapped all our turkeys to trade to other States for things like beavers.

One faction wanted to close the season until turkeys built back up again. Another said we should kill only one turkey each, until the population reconstituted itself — although most of this faction hadn't killed a turkey in four or five years

and were simply venting their spleen on those who had —
and half a dozen people agreed with whomever happened to
be talking at the time and spent the season jumping blithely
back and forth across the gap between illogic and unreason.

Fortunately, The Dictator, the member no hunting club
can do without, the man who says what you are not going
to do because he don't want to, and, furthermore, is the man
who can make it stick, told everybody to shut up, that turkeys were simply not gobbling, just like they didn't gobble in
the spring of 1924.

Nobody but he had been there in 1924, and since he had
both the rank and the authority to control the club, everybody went away grumbling, but at least they went away. Secretly, I didn't believe that business about 1924, either, but I
knew we still had turkeys, and since I had neither the rank,
the clout, nor the desire to foment a mutiny, I went off just
like everybody else, but quietly.

Any reservations I may have had about 1924 didn't bother
me at all. The Dictator was doing only what he had to do to
quell the revolt, doing what all commanders have to do from
time to time. If you question that, and if you still think George
Washington never told a lie in his life, go back and read his
general order to the Continental Army that accomplished the
retreat from Long Island in August 1776. Mark Twain would
have been proud of him.

We had an inventory this last year, thank God, because
it was the most silent season since 1968. That year has been
gone for twenty-seven years, but if you are trying to establish
a frequency of a quarter-century, I can't go back a quarter-
century before that and remember enough about the season
of 1941 to count. I know we had one, and I know I went as
often as someone would take me; but there were so few turkeys then, and it being only my third season, I had no basis
for comparison nor values to judge against.

ANTICIPATION

In 1941, everything connected with the whole business was a mystery. Now that I am older and much wiser, only half of it is.

This last year was strange, with or without a twenty-seven-year cycle.

It warmed up so early that I dropped the last ten days of the snipe season voluntarily. It felt too much like spring shooting. I am too weak on the migratory habits of snipe to offer any sensible comment at all. I don't know whether snipe follow isochronal migration lines, catch up to spring, or wait till late and go all the way up in one long leap. It doesn't matter. It just got warm early and stayed so warm that I convinced myself I was shooting girl snipe with fertilized egg cells, and I quit.

We didn't really have any river at all until the first week of March but we had tons of vegetation. By March 7th, the oaks had come into catkins, and the red maple was in fruit. Elm had been two weeks in flower already, and there was loblolly pollen on the car hood every morning. Cypress and dogwood had budded, the huckleberry was in full flower, and the willow was in leaf.

We were beginning to get myrtle warblers in flocks. Then, on the night of March 7th, we got 4 inches of rain in five hours, guaranteeing that the river was going to come out.

By March 9th, the Alabama River was at 41 feet at Claiborne — flood stage is 42 — and every station on the Tombigbee was above flood stage from Yellow Creek to the Alabama forks. Both rivers rose and fell without establishing any definite pattern. We had one day with a high of 74 degrees, although it was too windy to lay brick, and things shifted back and forth till March 15th.

That afternoon we got 4 inches of rain in two-and-a-half hours, a hailstorm that lasted for thirty minutes with stones the size of mothballs, and, at the conclusion of the hailstorm, a rainbow in the backyard.

Eight inches of rain in seven days, the last 4 inches falling in just two-and-a-half hours, guaranteed that opening day would be held along the beach at the edge of the backwater. The rainbow in the backyard qualified as the omen of the year.

2

OMENS AND THE RIVER

If I had the power to control the opinion of others, I would have you understand that I do not believe in luck. I would convince you that I conducted myself and all my affairs in a climate of creative anticipation, ready to seize the moment and catch the tide at every flood, eternally loaded and cocked, with the safety off.

Unfortunately, you can't fool any of the people any of the time with iron-assed pronouncements like that; and in addition to my inability to control opinion, I have another defect.

I am, after all, a descendant of those Celtic hill tribes who painted themselves with woad and worshiped pagan gods, and not all that long ago, either. There are things that make me uncomfortable. You could say, with considerable justice, if you chose, that I am superstitious about not being superstitious.

When a victorious general returned to Rome, if the victory had been one of sufficient magnitude, he was awarded a triumph. He was paraded through the streets, between the lines of cheering thousands, with the defeated enemy chieftains walking in chains behind his chariot, barefoot, with horse shit packed between their toes.

In the chariot with the general rode an augur, whose purpose it was to whisper continuously in his ear that in spite of the tumult and the cheering, he must remember that he was only a man, after all, and that Fortune often changed sides.

I have never been a general, and none of my triumphs have ever been witnessed by thousands, but Celts, unlike generals, need no augur. He is built in. He comes with the genes. We are uncomfortable without him.

Of those things not readily explainable, the whole field of the occult separates itself into several broad categories.

Those matters concerning information exchanges with persons who have crossed the line before us, such as seances, Ouija-board writing, crystal-ball reading, and ghostly apparitions, usually go on indoors and mostly require bad light. Things such as these are visions, usually requiring the assistance of a medium to interpret, or to do the faking, whichever side of the street you happen to be on, and generally concern themselves wholly with information passed back to us from beyond the divide.

Things that have automatic built-in penalties, like birds in the house, hats on the bed, opened umbrellas in the hall, or broken mirrors happen mostly indoors, but are not restricted to either day or night time frames and need no interpretations.

Omens that flow from nature, like new moons over the left shoulder, graveyard hants, freshly shot albatrosses, fiery crosses, or strange flocks of birds happen outside; and people like soldiers or bullfighters or druids or turkey hunters are the principal witnesses to such phenomena.

These I consider to be true omens, not all of which are invariable indicators of good or bad luck. Many of them lend themselves to individual interpretations and conclusions that can be totally erroneous.

There is still another category — that of the second sight, sometimes simply called "the sight" — that is a particular idiosyncrasy of the Celts. Many Celts are convinced they can foretell drownings, deaths, desertions, visitations of devils — all kinds of things that have an aura of doom about them — before they happen.

There appear to be very few visions of good luck before the fact. If there are, no one ever talks about them or is willing to admit to their existence.

Finally, there are the voices, which I readily admit to not being perfectly free of myself.

My grandmother used to say she could feel rabbits run over her grave, and I know exactly what she meant by it.

You may banish me to whatever intellectual penal colony you choose because of this, but I listen to little voices — and worse, I often do what they say.

I never, for instance, decide beforehand where I will hunt on opening day. I leave the house with a mind kept perfectly blank; or, if I have accepted an invitation to go somewhere that is unfamiliar, make no attempt to discover the lay of the land before the fact. Under ordinary circumstances, this is a serious mistake, because the most important part of hunting turkeys is the possession of an exhaustive knowledge of the land on which you hunt. But on opening day I prefer to trade skill and intelligence for ignorance and superstition and put my dependence in the little voices.

Something will turn me down the proper road. After it has sent me in the correct direction, I will continue to walk until something tells me to stop. There will be no bright lights; an angel will not visit with a flaming sword; the Ghost of Christmas Yet to Come will not appear and beckon with a spectral finger. But the little voices speak.

They can be wrong and often are, but the percentage of right to wrong is such that I seldom ignore the whispers deliberately, and, if I do, I generally pay for it later.

All these, of course, are tactical, operational voices. Omens are strategic. Omens are concrete signals evident and exhibited before the fact. Like the rainbow in the backyard after the hailstorm.

The thunderstorm of last March 15th, which gave us 4 inches of rain in two-and-a-half hours, closed with a substantial hailstorm. The size of the stones varied between that of 00 buckshot and mothballs, and there was no wind at all during the period of hail, which lasted for a solid thirty minutes. There was enough hail to drop the temperature rather quickly and drop it low enough to create a light ground fog after the sun came out, and leave enough ice to coat the deck behind the house with a solid sheet of hailstones.

After the clouds moved off to the southeast and the hail changed to a light drizzle, we had a rainbow in the backyard that began at the northeast corner of the playhouse, had an apogee of roughly 12 feet — you could have reached it with a fishing pole — and ended in the yard of the house next door. The maximum span of the arch would have been nearly 100 feet and the total width of the bands was about 18 inches. You could see both ends of it clearly, walk up to the arch at a point low enough to be within reach near either end, and put your hands into the colors.

If you backed up some 30 or 40 feet, the colors were bright and clear. Up close, literally at arm's reach, with your hands thrust into the bands, they were more ethereal, but still plain.

I regret to be compelled to report that there was no pot of gold at either end. I did not dig at either place but did probe with a steel rod at my end; and, since the neighbors next door were not home, trespassed on their property, strictly in the interests of science, of course, and probed there, too.

I had seen very minor rainbows in the spray from a garden hose or lawn sprinkler before — a curved dim band perhaps 3 feet across — and had of course seen the normal, lofty set of bands away up in the sky where, to quote Dorothy, "troubles melt like lemon drops."

I had never been close enough to touch a rainbow before, and the sensation was nothing less than magical. A child would have been enchanted. This wrinkled old man was as near enchantment as wrinkled old men can ever get.

It was there for probably twenty minutes and could have been there somewhat longer — I stepped out of the shop door and saw it already in full flower — and then, as the sun moved, it faded and was gone in a matter of fifteen seconds. When it faded away, you felt as if something had died.

I had been in the shop working on my portable blind at the time, sewing up a couple of tears in the camouflage material. If I were completely under the influence of old Irish mysticism, I would have taken the blind, rolled it up, and passed it through the colors rather than my hands, to put the magic on the equipment. But I did not.

Those of us who specialize in little voices have much less confidence in major superstitions like magical rainbows, swords buried in stones, or sheep intestines, but are afraid to disregard them.

A backyard rainbow, to one who steers his course by signs, has to be the omen of the year, and, one would think, be indicative of a forthcoming golden season.

From March 15th until March 19th, we were under the influence of what the weather bureau calls a cutoff low, which here on the coast means unusually warm weather, circulation out of the Gulf, and lots of rain. The Alabama River was just under flood stage at Claiborne and the Tombigbee above flood at every station south of Demopolis. There were falling stages at all points above that, but the rise would be three or four days coming down. We will have rises down here several days after falling stages 100 miles upriver.

The river comes and goes very quickly here, and especially in warm springs, with the vegetation so far advanced, turkeys in the river swamp are perfectly capable of staying in trees for two or three weeks, living on buds. I have never been able to find a rational reason for their doing that when other choices exist.

On the western end of the Alabama River cutoff, where the cutoff goes into the Tombigbee, it is a measured mile to the ridge behind Bates' Lake on the west bank.

I have seen turkeys fly three-quarters of a mile a good deal, seen them fly across the river often, and cannot imagine why they would spend three weeks in trees with dry land only a mile away. Dry land near enough to let you see the tops of the loblolly pine on Bates' Lake ridge, from the bank on the other side of the river.

In Edward A. McIlhenny's classic, *The Wild Turkey and Its Hunting,* he tells of Charles L. Jordan's seeing a flock that stayed in trees for two months, and he saw them from the window of his camp every day.

If a turkey has one single overriding quality it would probably be adaptability. During the floods we had in western Alabama in 1990, a biologist friend of mine saw turkeys in full strut in front of hens on the Fourth of July weekend. That year, there were yearling turkeys that weighed less than 5 pounds seen in the woods during the October deer season.

But that is necessity. The floods kept turkeys from nesting, or rising water destroyed nests already established, and turkeys simply waited out the flood and nested after it was gone, regardless of the date.

What keeps turkeys in trees over floodwaters, almost in sight of dry ground for two to three weeks or, in the case of Jordan's observation, for two months, cannot be necessity. Several times I have seen budding flocks in the spring, moving from tree to tree in a leisurely fashion, and the forward progress of the drove would be at about the speed a man would saunter, if he was in no special hurry and was looking over the timber or laying out a logging operation. They could cover 2 or 3 miles a day in this fashion, if they maintained the same direction.

They stay in trees through choice, not necessity, but the reason for such a choice is beyond me.

If you choose to disagree with my two- to three-week observation, considering it to be the vacant maunderings of an old man rather far gone in his cups, you are entitled to. And, of course, if you find my story too big to swallow, then you must find Jordan's observation of a flock that spent two months aloft to be perfectly preposterous.

Anything you choose to think about me is probably right. I am, at best, teetering along the ragged edge of senility, and the only drink I ever turned down in my life was because I misunderstood the question.

Charles L. Jordan is another kettle of fish altogether, and you disagree with him at your peril.

The Wild Turkey and Its Hunting, one of the earliest classics on turkey hunting, was written by Edward A. McIlhenny. In his introduction, he makes the point that he was not writing McIlhenny, he was writing Jordan. He came into possession of Jordan's manuscripts and papers after Jordan's death and compiled his book from them. In the introduction, McIlhenny says: "I have carried out the story of the wild turkey

as if told by Mr. Jordan, as his full notes on the bird enable
me to do this."

Two chapters early on in the book, "The Turkey Prehis-
toric" and "The Turkey Historic," were written by Dr. R. W.
Shufelt of Washington, D.C. The balance is Jordan, compiled
by McIlhenny. McIlhenny says so.

Jordan was born in Alabama in 1842, the youngest of three
brothers and the son of a hunting father. He began hunting
squirrels and other small game as a very small boy and took
up turkeys seriously at the age of sixteen, although he says he
had some earlier experiences. He hunted in Alabama, Mississippi, and Louisiana, between the Mississippi and Tombigbee
Rivers, and had some experience in Florida and east Texas.

Jordan's last ten years, from 1899 to 1909, were spent in
photography, and considering the equipment available at the
time and the difficulty of his subject, he was evidently calling
turkeys right up into his lap to be able to photograph them.

Jordan was killed by a poacher near Hammond, Louisiana, in early 1909. His career spanned the period from 1858
to 1909, a matter of more than fifty years, before game laws
or limits, largely before the lumber industry moved south,
and in an era when the total population of both Alabama and
Mississippi was less than 1.5 million.

Jordan was managing a game preserve when he was killed,
and throughout the book there is little evidence that he had
to do anything but hunt. Either he was independently well
off, or he managed to live as if he were.

There is no recording of scores in the book. But there is
a lot of evidence of big kills in throwaway lines like, "Seeing two gobblers put their heads together at about forty yards
from me, I fired, killing both. The flock flew in all directions.
One hen passed within twenty paces of me and I killed it
with the second barrel."

And, "As I had three turkeys already in my boat, I felt no desire to molest them as I drifted by and under them."

Forty turkeys a year for fifty years is 2,000 turkeys.

Surely Jordan was there. Very probably he was substantially beyond that. The fact that he never bothers to add it up tells you that he didn't give it a lot of thought.

It also tells you that unless you think he deliberately intended to mislead, he ought to be listened to. I know there is such a thing as experienced incompetence, but who do you know who can speak from the eminence of 2,000 turkeys?

If Charles L. Jordan says he saw a drove of gobblers spend two months in the trees over a river swamp, I am convinced. To me, the fact that I have never had an opportunity to see it does not mean that it does not happen.

Jordan was, in many ways, light-years ahead of his time. Thirty years ago, the book said you had to have unbroken areas of at least 5,000 acres of mature timber to have turkeys. Somewhere around the turn of the century — now nearly a hundred years ago — Jordan wrote:

> There are thousands of acres in the South which were once cultivated, but which are now abandoned and growing up with timber, brush, and grass. Such country affords splendid opportunity for the rearing and perpetuation of the wild turkey. These lands are vastly superior for this purpose than are the solid primeval forests, inasmuch as they afford a great variety of summer food, such as green, tender herbage, berries of many kind, grasshoppers by the million, and other insects in which turkeys delight. Such a country also affords good nesting retreats, with brier-patches and straw where the nest may be safely hidden, and where the young birds may secure safe hiding places from animals and birds

of prey; but alas! not from trappers, batters, and pot hunters. Check these, and the abandoned plantations of the South would soon be alive with turkeys.

Sounds like Dan Speake in 1980 or George Hurst in 1991, rather than some of the garbage that was accepted as gospel in 1960, and is still the official doctrine in some barbershops I know of today.

To my knowledge, Jordan was the first who talked about the late-fall separation into droves by age and sex, and the first to say that hens do not call gobblers but that gobblers call hens, an opinion still not held by about 90 percent of the people hunting today.

I have heard comments to the effect that if Jordan was still with us, he wouldn't do as well today. He believed in the rifle, and used it to the end, which gave him the advantage of the toughest 40 yards of all, that area between 80 yards out and 40 yards out, when turkeys can see you best. You make the most mistakes there and run more turkeys off there — waiting them out in the gap from in sight to in range. It is the hardest part of all, and a man with a rifle can pull the trigger at 85 yards and save himself the dirty end of this stick.

On the other hand, Jordan spent his last ten years with an 1890 camera, and to get the pictures that he did, had to have been calling turkeys into bayonet range.

It reminds me of the story of when Ted Williams and Ty Cobb were conducting their media debate as to which era had the better hitters, and Cobb was asked what did he think he would hit against modern pitching. He said probably somewhere in the neighborhood of .320. When the reporter commented that this was a low number for a man with a lifetime average of .367, who had never been particularly noted for his modesty, Cobb said, "That's true. But then you have to remember that I am nearly sixty-eight years old."

OMENS AND THE RIVER

Take the next couple of months off and invent a time machine, go back and get Jordan and Cobb in their respective primes, and bring them up to 1995, and I suspect we might find it both interesting and instructive.

In 1995, without the presence of Mr. Jordan to advise us, the season started with both the Alabama and Tombigbee Rivers in flood, and the ground I normally hunt having the 25 percent of it that is river bottomland under 6 feet of water.

I don't know how many turkeys had come ashore, or how many elected to stay in trees over the water and tough it out. For those that chose to stay, it couldn't have been all that tough, because the backwater was gone by the end of the first week, and all the oak was in full catkin, along with the willow. The hack-berry, yellow poplar, and sweet gum were in small leaf. Any turkey that wanted to spend ten days budding could do it easily, either over the water or over dry ground, wherever he happened to be when the flood came.

As far as I was concerned, the matter was academic. For the first time since 1940, I was going to start the season out of the state, in central Florida, near what later came to be known as Paynes Prairie, but what William Bartram called the Alachua Savannah, when he visited there in 1774.

3

PAYNES PRAIRIE

William Bartram, the Philadelphia naturalist, made several visits to the Southeast in the late eighteenth century. After failing as a merchant's apprentice in Philadelphia, he first came south in 1761, to visit his Uncle William on the Cape Fear River in North Carolina. He set up a store there and stayed until 1765, when his father, John Bartram, who had just been appointed botanist to King George III, came through on his way to Florida. William, whose business was not prospering, abandoned it and went with his father to Florida as a volunteer assistant, serving without pay.

Bartram remained in Florida after his father returned to Philadelphia, growing rice and indigo on the St. John's River until 1767. He went broke in the rice business in 1767, went back to Philadelphia, failed again in the mercantile business in 1770, and revisited Uncle William at Cape Fear and hung around there until 1772, when he came home again to Philadelphia, now either O-for-4, or O-for-5, depending on how you want to score the abandonment of his first apprenticeship in 1761.

It appears that none of this was due to a lack of anything but interest. Bartram seems to have been unable to submerge his fascination with nature long enough to make a living.

Bartram returned south in 1773, commissioned by Dr. John Fothergill of London, with the following instructions:

"It will be right to keep a little journal, marking the soil, situation, plants in general, remarkable animals, where found, and the several particulars relative to them as they cast up. . . . Mark the places the plants grow in, under shade or in the open country."

His salary was to be 50 pounds a year, with additional allowances for expenses and for the drawings to be made. He was now thirty-four years old, and I suspect that his father was delighted to have him out of the house, gainfully employed, at least two jumps in front of the sheriff, and, hopefully, out from underfoot for some time to come.

Bartram set sail for Charleston in 1773 and did not return to Philadelphia till 1777. The account of those four years of travel by boat, horse, and foot, down the southern colonies as far south as Orlando and as far west as the Mississippi River, is what gave us the *Travels,* published in 1791, established his reputation as the premier botanist in the American colonies, and, after thirty-four years on the awkward squad, constituted a double off the wall with the bases loaded.

In 1773, as best you can tell from the times and distances noted, somewhere in Clay County, Florida, on his way to the Alachua Savannah, Bartram wrote:

> Having rested very well during the night, I was awakened in the morning early, by the cheering converse of the wild turkey-cock *(Meleagris occidentalis)* saluting each other, from the sun-

brightened tops of the lofty *Cypressus disticha* and *Magnolia grandiflora.* They begin at early dawn, and continue till sun rise, from March to the last of April. The high forests ring with the noise, like the crowing of the domestic cock, of these social sentinels, the watch-word being caught and repeated, from one to another, for hundreds of miles around; insomuch that the whole country, is for an hour or more, in a universal shout.

In nearby Alachua County is the Alachua Savannah, later called Paine's Prairie, clearly one of Bartram's favorite pieces of terrain. His lyrical description of it was extracted and used in the general announcement of the proposed publication of the *Travels* in late 1790.

This last year, I opened the spring season of 1995 in the same general area that Bartram described.

The aspect of the country has changed since 1773, and I did not hear as many turkeys there the morning of March 21, 1995, as Bartram did, 222 years earlier, in the same month. But there were enough. I have some inflammatory remarks to make about what kind they were later on, but if there has ever been an example of the innate ability of a turkey to adapt to the conditions at hand, this place takes both ears and the tail.

Traveling east on Interstate 10, there are two pronounced changes in terrain and ground cover as you go away from Pensacola. The first 100 miles is generally through sterile Norfolk sands that run heavily to blackjack and turkey oak, with a skimpy scattering of sand pine. Most of these are xeric, barren, low-site sand hills. There are some pictures on file of 300-year-old, virgin longleaf on these sites that can't be more than 14 inches in diameter.

From about Quincy to Tallahassee, the land becomes a

mixture of pine and hardwood, heavier to pine, but not bad-looking habitat at all. As you go south from 1-10, toward Lake City and south of there, you leave the mixed pine-and-hardwood stands and come to the palmetto belt.

There is a coastal strip between 50 and 100 miles wide, through all the South Atlantic states, that nearly has the market cornered in palmetto. It exists, sometimes pure and sometimes mixed in with gallberry, in stands almost too thick to break through and almost thick enough to lie on top of. There are places in heavy palmetto/gallberry understory where, if you fell, you wouldn't go all the way down. Somewhere at about a 45-degree angle, you would be propped up by the vegetation. From the time you leave the road in there, your legs become invisible from the knees down.

Back in the days of old-growth longleaf, when the country burned over annually, fires kept the understory reasonably in check.

Nowadays, with as much planted Slash as there is, and as good as wildfire protection has become, the understory should be controlled with prescribed burns. Unfortunately, Florida is almost as bad as California in its policy of conducting Forest Management by Ignorance, and the county oversight boards, which have roughly the power of a federal judge, or a beat commissioner in Mississippi, control forest management in Florida in precisely the same manner that Tomas Torquemada handled the Spanish Inquisition. You can get a controlled-burn permit in Florida just about as easily as you can get a permit to dig in the yard at Fort Knox. Which means you would have to catch an extremely highly placed official in bed with two boys, in either case.

The tract I had been invited to hunt left me absolutely without encouragement on the way into the camp house, and driving over the road net for a quick reconnaissance before roost time positively broke my heart.

Years ago, when hunting a new kind of game, or hunting in strange territory, or both, I formed the habit of keeping my mouth firmly shut. Nobody likes to hear a series of what he considers to be penetrating questions from a rookie hunter of anything from hummingbirds to elephants when, after the first question, every syllable out of the new guy's mouth turns over a fresh stone of stupidity.

Stay shut up, and it takes them longer to find out how dumb you really are.

I stayed shut up, but it wasn't easy.

It appeared evident at the time that we had just driven 500 miles, and abandoned as good a place to hunt turkeys as there is east of the Mississippi River, to spend three days wading through armpit-deep palmetto. Any man alive today who has been hunting turkeys since 1938 has certainly crossed over the crest and is on the far slope. He cannot have all that many opening days left, and he damned sure ain't got enough left to waste one of them, let alone pound it down a rathole.

I didn't waste one. The place was and is full of turkeys. I just didn't know it at the time.

That first afternoon, we didn't hunt. That part of Florida closes the woods to hunting after noon, and all you can do is prowl and look and try to roost something. I was a long way from having any optimism at all that first afternoon, but I went at it as if I really expected to roost something, and I did it for a particular reason.

There is an unwritten rule that governs what you do when you hunt with nice people, and it is unwritten because it does not need to be formalized.

The square set knows instinctively that you give the guest the best you have; and if he is not only a guest, but is one of the old guys, you give him the best of the best. I had done this for years as a matter of course. Recently, I have come to enjoy

both sides of the offer because, usually, there is nobody older
on the ground.

My hosts were turkey hunters. They knew all the rules,
they were clearly giving me the best they had, and I was ob-
ligated to take it seriously.

Consequently, I took the territory they awarded me that
first afternoon and worked it as if, at any minute, I expected
an infuriated turkey to burst from his thicket and charge.

I found some tracks in the road — not many, but a few. At
the back of a green patch planted at the end of a logging road
there was a primary feather, either number V or number VI,
that had been knocked out very recently. On both sides of an
intermittent run of water a foot wide and an inch deep, in a
couple of acres where the Slash saplings were thick enough
to shade out the palmetto, I found a little scratching in the
pine straw.

It sort of reminded you of 1955. A far cry from the analogy
of the sultan's son on his first night in the harem, who only
need concern himself with where to start, but not hopeless.

Maybe poor and scrawny, maybe pretty thin on the ground,
but there, definitely, something there.

That night, over the bourbon, we got to talking about the
ground.

You talk to professional woodsmen, still in the business,
and you get a real feel of the characteristics of the land.

The place is about 7,000 acres, virtually all of it in Slash-
pine plantations on a twenty-five-year rotation, with a heavy
understory of palmetto and gallberry. About 3 percent of
the tract is hardwood, 200 acres more or less; but, as far as I
could see, almost without an oak tree on it. There is no dogwood, almost no sweet gum, and the hardwood is principally
a mixture of black gum and sweet bay. All the hardwood is
small, and it is all restricted to narrow bands along intermittent streams.

Managing a tract like this, on a twenty-five-year rotation that has been in effect long enough to go completely over the tract at least once, means that at all times, there will be roughly 300 acres recently clear-cut and waiting to be planted, 300 acres in the process of being cut, 300 acres that have seedlings one year old, and probably another 300 acres in trees between knee and crotch high. Allowing 150 acres in roads and, assuming you feel generous, about 300 acres without a heavy understory, you tally up less than 2,000 acres out of 7,000 suitable for forage, and this includes the roads.

Considering the ground cover and the seed sources, the roads may be the best of all.

But a turkey can fly over any part of it he chooses. While I have no chemical analysis available to back up the statement, the air is perfectly breathable and appears just as capable of supporting flight as does the air in other, more favorable habitat of my experience.

One of the club members, who hunts this tract probably twenty days out of a thirty-five-day season, said that at the close of the season in 1994, there were thirty-six gobbling turkeys still at large and still on the tract. He could locate them on the map.

I certainly believe he could do this, and I do not believe he was stretching the truth.

I hunt very regularly in an area in Alabama that comprises 5,000 acres. At the close of a spring season there, I can count every gobbling turkey and can locate him on the map accurately enough to kill him with battalion volleys of 155mm artillery.

There is nothing unusual in this. In *The Wild Turkey and Its Hunting,* Charles Jordan talks about knowing droves of gobblers with a degree of familiarity that enabled him to tell if one was missing. Any careful old-line turkey hunter can do the same thing. And before you spend the money to call the Alabama Game and Fish Division and turn me in, we do not, at my club, shoot turkeys with battalion, two volleys of 155s.

As a matter of fact, I don't actually know of a club that does, although that bunch across Pine Log Creek, who religiously bait our turkeys across the line every February, is certainly capable of doing so.

If you use the rule of thumb that there are five turkeys that do not gobble, because of either age or sex, for every one that does, it means that this 7,000 acres of pine flatwoods in Florida has a population of 180 birds, or one every 38 acres, a figure clearly up in the "good" category.

It would be more comfortable if you don't ask me what these turkeys eat. I can't tell you. I can report only that they eat something because they surely don't have pizza sent out from Lake City.

I killed a turkey the first morning. Nothing gobbled in hearing in any direction and, strangest of all, I didn't hear a single owl. The locals say they don't hear owls much; maybe they are allergic to palmetto. But I prowled the roads and hawked, and cawed, and hooted, and finally, because it was too early to quit, made like it was 1955 all over again and went and sat over the scratching along the little run I had found the afternoon before.

Fifteen minutes after I got there, after I had yelped twice, a three-year-old gobbler that weighed maybe 17 pounds walked up, obligingly put his head behind a tree so I could get my gun off my knee, then stepped around the tree and joined his ancestors.

He was hog fat, was perfectly healthy and in good plumage, and was wholly and completely unearned.

The account squared itself the next morning — there is an invariable rule that it always will — when I earned one I didn't get.

This one began to gobble at daylight and kept it up at intervals regular enough to leave you in no doubt as to either direction or distance. He was near enough to the road I had walked in on so that I could use it to get back to him and he was off the road, maybe 150 yards, and on the edge of one of the little hardwood runs. In the half-dark, it looked as if the ground along the little creek was open enough for him to walk in on, so I stepped off the road on his side, moved around the bushes that grew up along the roadside, and set up.

He gobbled several times after I had sat down, at the same interval between gobbles he had been using since I first heard him, and when I yelped one time, cut me off before I could finish.

With familiar turkeys, I will shut up at this point, and pretty well stay shut up, so I did the same thing with him. I didn't hear anything fly down, though I was surely close enough to hear anything but sailing down, when he gobbled again some 30 yards south of where he was the first time. Thinking he had simply dropped down silently, I was concentrating on the ground along the little creek when a turkey left his limb, flew past me at a range of 5 yards, and pitched down in the road behind me. He was so close you could hear his feet thump when he landed in the road.

If someone had told you before the fact that a turkey would leave the limb in front of you and fly past at long fishing-pole range when you said "pull," it would have been an easy shot, a straightforward high-house target from Station 7, only requiring that you not let it get too close before you shot.

Only nobody had said anything before the fact. The turkey surprised me by coming from the wrong direction and wasn't on the ground, and I wasn't ready for him yet.

While I was sitting there, trying to think of some clever way to riposte, wondering if the screen of bushes between the turkey in the road and me was thick enough for me to turn around and still thin enough to see through — both highly unlikely, the second turkey, which hadn't left the limb at all, pitched out, followed the same flight pattern as the first one, and landed in the road behind me with a louder thump than the first had made.

Having been given an identical second chance, I was even more unprepared for it than I had been for the first chance.

No incompetence in existence can hold a candle to experienced incompetence, and that is the deepest cut of all.

There had been two turkeys all along. When I thought the first one had flown down because the gobble seemed to come from a different place, I had been wrong. It had come from a different place because it had come from a different turkey, then gobbling for the first time.

The two of them were now standing in the road, 10 yards behind me, safely home and dry. By twisting my neck and straining my right eye almost out of its corner, I could get an occasional glimpse of feathers through the thick bushes. There was no way to jump up and turn around, no way to ease around, no way they were coming back in front of me. I gave them fifteen minutes, and when there was no further sound and I could not see anything out of the corner of my eye, I eased up, crept out to the edge of the road, and looked over the bushes.

They were 150 yards up the road, with necks stretched out as long as hoe handles, looking back toward where they had landed, with suspicion oozing from every pore.

The movement of my head over the bushes put them into one of those 10-mile-an-hour trots they specialize in, and they disappeared around a curve in the road.

I hadn't deserved the second chance. Clearly, there was not going to be a third.

Another turkey was killed by our party that morning, and one had been killed the day before.

All three were in good shape. I saw two of them picked, and both were full of yellow fat. The breast sponge was full and normal. There is not enough agriculture in this region to count. There is no feeding program and few green patches.

These turkeys are making it in pine flatwoods, in timber being grown on a twenty-five-year rotation, in an understory thick enough so that large portions of it are simply too thick for a turkey to do anything but hide in, without dogwood, without oak, without even pitcher-plant flats to grow crawfish in.

Palmetto in season has a stalk of small berries, and in the fall robins come in droves that look like smoke to eat gallberries. Black-gum fruits are here, but not many, because there are not many black-gum trees, and twenty-five-year-old slash pine has cones and seeds, but they aren't much to eat.

Before this trip, if you had taken me down there and offered me the whole 7,000 acres — to own, not just to hunt — I would have shaken your hand, thanked you profusely, mentally decided to send you a ham every Christmas, and, as soon as you left, gotten to a real-estate firm as quickly as possible to sell the property so I could use the proceeds to buy a place to hunt turkeys in mixed stands of hardwood and loblolly pine.

But not now. Now I have seen the elephant. Now I believe. If you choose to tell me that turkeys can make it in abandoned coal mines, or old, empty warehouses down on the docks, or around the rims of active volcanoes, I will not disagree. Everything I thought I knew about turkeys went out the window.

I find I am immensely lighter from the ears up.

4

OSCEOLA?

One of the advantages of having appeared in print in national magazines is that you get to meet a lot of nice people; and usually, after a person has read your stuff for a while, he begins to feel as if he knows you, and will write and be pretty familiar with what he says.

I have never objected to this, and I do not now. Very probably an assessment of your character, based on what you write, is accurate. I have held for years that people are eventually going to find out what you are. Good or bad, pleasant or indifferent, it will ultimately come out; for the same reason that no man can be a hero to either his wife or his secretary. They have seen too much of him. There are no more secrets. They know that in most cases the clay goes all the way up to the knees. Show up in print enough, and you give your readers the same opportunity.

The only trouble with longtime readers knowing so much

about you is that in certain instances you become family. And once you get to be family, they can say anything to you they like. Nothing is sacred, for there is no cide like fratricide.

They will often ask for advice, and if you are unable to give it, they will become irritated. They do not believe it is a shortage of knowledge. They think it is a refusal to share, and refusal breaches their comfort threshold.

Because we live in both a goal-oriented and a record-keeping society, certain things take on an importance that is badly overdrawn. It is really not of all-absorbing importance that such and such a left fielder has stolen more bases on Thursdays than any base runner since Max Carey, nor that a certain quarterback's completion percentage after six years is 10 points better than Bart Starr's was at the same time.

But we do this, and we keep up with it, and keep score on it, and we let it bother us.

There is a new fashion in turkey hunting called the grand slam. This means that a person has killed one specimen of each of the commonly accepted subspecies of wild turkeys in one season. Spring only, fall doesn't count, and they usually leave out the ocellated turkey in Mexico and restrict it to the four in the contiguous forty-eight.

I ain't into this. I never have been. I have killed only one turkey out of the state in my life, and when someone calls and asks my advice on the grand slam, I tell him right off I can't help.

I point out that there are lots of turkeys within 50 miles of my house that are perfectly capable of embarrassing me. That I can get my feelings hurt at the end of an hour's drive, and find it unnecessary to drive 400 miles to be humiliated, outthought, and walked around. The home folks do it beautifully; I don't need to give my business to strangers.

In fact, I have a rather strange opinion, not founded in

education, but founded partly in the inherent mistrust engendered by almost fifty years of buying timber.

I ain't all that sure there really are four subspecies to grand-slam with.

Right now I am reasonably sure of what is going through your mind.

Quote.

Here is this clown, clearly in the last tottering stages of his dotage, who has spent all his life looking up in a pine tree, acting like he thinks he is a taxonomist. He makes statements based on reasons founded in ignorance, redneck superstition, and, conceivably, even voodoo.

Edward Gibbon was right. If there is a chance that Rome fell because of brain damage in the intelligentsia caused by using pewter dishes for years, look what can happen to the thought processes of somebody who sucked on lead turkey yelpers for almost half a century. He ought to go and call the old soldiers' home in Biloxi right now, and reserve a rocker on a shady corner of the front porch. He surely needs to stay out of the sun while he rocks and drools the rest of the way to the boneyard.

Maybe.

And maybe not.

Take hold of the reins with both hands just for a minute and listen.

Taxonomists habitually fall into two broad categories. One of these groups is called "lumpers" and the other, "splitters."

Lumpers take the position that there are regional variations in weight, appearance, overall size, and the general makeup of things in nature, depending largely on climate and latitude.

The appearance of leaves on a black-locust tree, for instance, is substantially different in Alabama than the appearance of the same species in Pennsylvania. Deer in Maine out-weigh the white-tails of the Gulf Coast by about 70 pounds. If you have a professional eye, the families of slash pine in forest-tree seed orchards, collected across a five- or six-state area and then planted next to one another in the genetics area, look so different that you are tempted to say that an error has occurred, that some of this slash is loblolly.

Lumpers see this variation, file it under the category of interesting but not significant, and continue to call them black locust, and slash pine, and white-tailed deer, recognizing there are some minor regional characteristics.

Splitters, blown by the winds of change, and with an overweening desire to get their names in print, act like those people who stand in the mouths of alleys and sell you those oriental scarves with the sixty-eight different positions of lovemaking printed on them. The only difference between positions 34 and 35 is that in number 35 somebody's fingers are crossed.

Now that the Endangered Species Act has taken on the same characteristics as Moses' tablets or the Bill of Rights, splitters are crossing their fingers in all directions. These are the people who have had the Louisiana black bear declared a separate and endangered species, even though he is the genetic footprint of the Michigan black bear, the Maine black bear, and the Florida black bear.

Splitters are the people who have managed to get the 20,000 acres on Highway 10, between Pascagoula and Gulfport, Mississippi, declared a refuge for the Mississippi sandhill crane. The brochure they give you when you visit this area says that the total population of the refuge is 190 birds, that three-quarters of these come from eggs gathered in other areas and released at Gulfport, and that many of these releases have now entered into the breeding population.

If you were simpleminded enough to believe that this minor group of birds were truly a unique species to begin with, then this introduction of outside specimens has certainly adulterated the gene pool, and they have all been turned into a population of hybrids.

If any of this makes you want to rend your garments and send for your sackcloth and ashes, you should be aware that 300 miles west of Gulfport, in Katy, Texas, sandhill cranes are considered a game bird, there is an open season with a daily limit of three, and the season is handled by exactly the same Fish and Wildlife Service we have right here in the United States.

I am prepared to believe that there are land snails that exist on islands in the Everglades that, through centuries of isolation, have evolved into separate species on areas as small as 100 acres. The Galapagos Islands cover only 2,869 square miles and are loaded with species found nowhere else on earth.

But to tell me that a bird that can fly 40 miles an hour and exists across the entire sweep of the Gulf Coast can sit in one 20,000-acre area and evolve itself into a separate species slices the ham substantially thicker than I am willing to swallow.

The fact that the same Fish and Wildlife Service that manages the refuge also sets the seasons and limits on the population just across the line in Texas, tells me that this particular article of separatist faith is not accepted as infallible dogma by all their clergy. Someone other than me must be having trouble with the thickness of the slices.

Refer to William Bartram, who came across our end of the world in 1775 — the earliest professional eye we had looking at this country — and read what he says on page 260 of the *Naturalist's Edition of Bartram's Travels,* edited and annotated by Francis Harper:

Set off in the morning and in the course of the

day's journey crossed several creeks and brooks, one of which swam the horses. On passing by a swamp at the head of a bay or lagoon of the river, I observed a species of cypress; it differs a little from the white cedar of New Jersey and Pennsylvania *(Cupressus thyoides),* the trunk is short and the limbs spreading horizontally, the branches fuller of leaves and the cones larger and of a crimson or reddish purple color when ripe.

Bartram set off from the plantation of Major Robert Farmer and traveled north up the east side of the Alabama River. The "creek that swam the horses" was almost surely the Little River, the boundary between Baldwin and Monroe Counties, Alabama. There is nothing on this side of the river deep enough to do that to a horse for another 60 miles.

Cupressus thyoides, the name Bartram gave to the white cedar, was changed subsequently to *Chamaecyparis thyoides,* taking it out of the genus *Cupressus* and putting it into *Chamaecyparis,* but the point to be taken here is the accuracy of the man's eye.

From the back of a moving horse, he sees a tree that he last saw two years ago in New Jersey, with a thousand miles and God knows how many thousand specimens between the sightings, and detects a difference instantly.

And leaves it at that.

Doesn't claim a new species, which he does at other places in his writings; doesn't stake out a claim and file the papers to change the name of the tree to *Cupressus bartramii;* simply notes a regional difference, "a species of cypress that differs a little."

There is, of course, a move afoot now to declare this one a separate species. It has been carried as *Chamaecyparis thyoides,* Atlantic white cedar, for years, but now the splitters have their hatchets out and there is a proposal to change the name to *Chamaecyparis henryae,* Henry white cedar, in honor of its discoverer, Mrs. Mary G. Henry of Gladwyne, Pennsylvania, now deceased, who came to the party 200 years after Bartram.

As soon as this can be done then, obviously, the next step will be to declare this rare jewel to be endangered, have a scientific study decide that the presence of diesel fumes in the atmosphere inhibits its growth, and move to forbid all logging within 5 miles, air line, of every known specimen of Henry white cedar south of Montgomery, Alabama.

If you find that supposition overdrawn and unnecessarily sarcastic, go talk to any veteran of the spotted-owl stupidity in northern California.

But to return to the thesis I abandoned in order to become waspish, an eye that could detect differences in the characteristics of a species of *thyoides,* across such a gap of observations, would surely detect a difference in the appearance of the wild turkeys he saw in Gray Country, Florida, and the ones he saw later on in middle Alabama and earlier in upper Georgia and South Carolina.

The single Osceola I have to my credit, and the other two I saw the same day, could be put down in the middle of a string of Alabama turkeys 200 yards long and nobody alive could detect the difference.

The textbook *The Wild Turkey and Its Management,* published by the Wildlife Society, and now nearly thirty years old, is very firm in its contention that there are six subspecies, not four, adding Gould's and Mexican to the four we are now using. Killing all six in one year undoubtedly constitutes a grand slam in spades, doubled and redoubled, with the opponents vulnerable and, if you ran down to Yucatan and shot an ocellated to boot, there would be a bronze statue of you on your horse, waving a sword, in the town square.

Throw into the pot the Intergrade, the mixture of Florida
and Eastern that is supposed to occur from South Carolina
to Louisiana, add those absolutely-pure-as-a-West-Virginia-
ham specimens from coastal South Carolina so beloved by
Henry E. Davis and Archibald Rutledge (Rutledge insists his
had black heads), season with a soupçon of the legendary
mossyhead stories so beloved of your grandfather s era, and
we have the count up to eleven.

Enough to run completely out of descriptive adjectives
and to wear the numbers off three air travel cards belong-
ing to the citizen crisscrossing North America trying to get a
specimen of each.

I have asked the board for a ruling on someone who killed
one Florida and one Eastern in the same spring. Does such a
person qualify for a little slam?

The request for clarification remains unanswered.

I think we have let the whole thing get completely out of
hand, but if you are into this, if the field of pseudo-taxonomy
warms your id at its coals, you are entitled. Whatever floats
your boat.

We have a wild turkey. Audubon, Bartram, and Alexan-
der Wilson all described one. In a hundred pictures, you see
turkeys killed in open country in western states with nearly
white tips to their tail feathers and light-colored rump and
upper-tail coverts, and I am prepared to stipulate that neither
Audubon nor Bartram nor Wilson ever saw a Western turkey,
nor do I intend to imply that there have been no competent
biologists since John Audubon died in 1851. The present
generation just makes me a little uneasy in its avid preoccu-
pation with ink.

I admit to being a lumper, rather than a splitter, because I
feel we tend to stay off the lunatic fringe a trifle longer.

I feel heartily sorry for Mr. Gould, whoever he was, who
had a turkey named after him thirty years ago and who now

appears to be bereft, and I am well aware that I just served up an entire serving of ignorance and superstition, admitting guilt at both the beginning and end of it.

On the other hand, you can dissect humor to look at its bones and take the funny out of it. You can undertake, one afternoon, to show somebody how to kill doves, crossing left to right, picking your swing apart to exhibit its vertebra; and when you get through with the instruction, you are not only missing left to rights, you couldn't hit a barn if you were locked inside with the windows nailed shut.

There is no need to turn turkey hunting into an inferior imitation of those rump sessions in tactics, now so beloved by human-resource types, where groups of people sit around tables for twenty hours a week, writing on flip charts and looking for the final 5 percent of an impossible solution to an imaginary problem. Not only do they not find it, they frequently degrade what they already have down to 88 percent.

We already have a wild turkey, whatever subspecies he happens to be, and he is still getting the side out.

Let the kid pitch.

5

THE OTHER END
OF THE CURVE

Four days into the season, and 30 miles north of any pos-
sibility of finding a gallberry patch, I opened the home
season, in a timber type and on terrain that was all the way
at the other end of the bell curve from the central Florida
flatwoods. I opened it in eighty-five-year-old mixed stands of
pine and hardwood, on rolling ground in the upper coastal
plain, with a light understory held well under control by a
regular burning program. This is the way a great deal of the
world in this country used to look.

In a lot of places, when I say that, people ask me how I can
say it, because I wasn't here then. I can say it because I know
it, because we all know it. There is ample evidence available
if you know where to look for it, and the evidence shows that
a lot of the world did not look as we have come to imagine or
hypothesize that it did.

In the first place there are enormous collections of photographs.

The lumber industry didn't move south to any large extent until the white pine was cut out in the Lake States in the early 1890s and we do not have the soil to attract farmers.

Except for a few scattered areas of good land, the Southeast in general cannot compare in soil fertility with places like Ohio, Indiana, Illinois, and western Kentucky. The glacier that scraped all the topsoil off the Laurentian Shield in Canada deposited it along the terminal moraine, which didn't get this far. That moraine was 600 miles north of here. Consequently, the small farmers who took advantage of the land disposals after the American Revolution migrated there, into an area of 40-foot topsoil.

With minor exceptions, there was no large-scale farming in the South. The biggest change in the aspect of this land came after the timber industry moved here in 1900. Ample photographs exist from the late 1880s and early 1900s to give us a good idea of the look of a lot of the timber, and the method used to make the Public Land Survey at the beginning of the nineteenth century gives us some hard numbers on almost all of it.

All of the United States, with the exception of the thirteen original colonies, and some minor French and Spanish land grants along rivers in the Gulf States, was covered by the Public Land Survey, begun after the Revolution.

The land was surveyed by contract surveyors, and was laid out in townships and ranges, with 36 sections to the township and each section, a mile square, having 640 acres. As the survey crews ran the lines of these sections, they described the characteristics of the land traversed. The unit of measure in use then was the chain, a distance of 66 feet. As archaic as it seems today, it was — and is — a handy yardstick. There are 80 chains to the mile, 40 to the half, 20 to a quarter, and 10 square chains make an acre.

Rural land all over the United States is still bought and sold on these measurements and this description.

The General Land Office for Alabama and a lot of Mississippi was in Huntsville, Alabama, and survey crews for both states were headquartered and controlled from there.

They kept what are called field notes as they went, platted the sections as they were surveyed. A typical set of field notes for a section would read as follows:

> Left NE corner Sec. 10, T 2 N, Rn 2 E, running South; at 15 chains crossed creek running SW. At 18 chains entered cane, at 30 chains and 50 links, left cane. Set Quarter post at 40 chains. Set Mile-post at 80 chains from whence:

N 35°E	35 links	14 inch Pine
S 40°E	45 links	12 inch Pine
S 60°W	20 links	18 inch Pine
N 55°W	80 links	8 inch Oak

> Land rolling to hilly with moderate growth of third-rate timber.

These notes were kept in longhand. The originals are still on file in Washington, D.C., but almost all county courthouses keep copies in the tax assessor's office.

Alabama's lines were run from about 1810 to 1825 or so, nearby states around the same time, though not much before 1800, but in all cases, before any appreciable amount of timber was cut.

Except for personal use, the theft of some big cypress along the river, and some minor cutting that was floated down streams, the timber the Public Land Survey crews looked at in 1814 was the timber here when Columbus landed.

The witness trees they tallied around each milepost (section corner) were the nearest trees in each of the four quadrants of the circle, the tree's diameter and direction, its species, and its distance from the corner in links. (A link is 1/1000 of a chain.)

We have then, on record, four one-quarter circular plots of known radii, even though the plots vary in size, the size of the tree in each plot, and its species, at 35 locations in the township. This comes to a total of 140 plots per township, which makes a perfectly legitimate timber cruise.

The pine stands in this part of Alabama stood 136 trees per acre with an average diameter of 16 inches. Beneath them, as an understory, were 3 hardwood trees per acre with an average diameter of 10 inches.

I love to be asked the question,

"How do you know what was here originally?"

Because it enables me to answer,

"I know because us taxpayers had it cruised."

The numbers I just quoted are, of course, averages; when you get to digging into the data, the field notes, it becomes obvious that the whole timber stand was a hodgepodge.

Although the accuracy decreases as you consider smaller and smaller samples, it is plain that there were stands in excess of 20,000 feet per acre, as well as areas where, for two or three section corners in a row, the nearest tree was a chain to a chain and a half out from the corner, with volumes of 1,000 feet per acre.

The last glacier receded some 10,000 years ago. It was some 600 miles between south Alabama and the edge of the ice then. Whatever was here at the time, probably spruce and fir, but maybe open steppe, you can guarantee it was not longleaf.

Longleaf matures and dies in about 350 years on these soils. Give things a couple of hundred years to warm up after the ice, and you have time for some thirty separate generations of longleaf to come in, mature, die out, and come again. The whole 70 million acres did not all seed at once, grow and die at once, if for no other reason than the time it took for temperature to change across the 600 miles as the ice receded.

It seeded in as a mixed jumble, lived and died as one for 9,900 years, and was still one when the lumber industry left Michigan and came south in 1900.

Longleaf occurs in even aged stands, and the mixture was not spread evenly across every acre; but there was clearly a wider spread of ages and sizes than we have fooled ourselves into thinking there was. It did not stand 15,000 feet per acre from Virginia to Texas.

There is no intention on my part to demean the central Florida flatwoods. You hunt on what you have. But the difference in appearance between unburned palmetto/gallberry flats, and lower Clarke County, Alabama, is immense.

Not only do you see your feet, you can see the feet of someone 200 yards away, unless he happens to be standing over a little hill and is consequently invisible from the knees down.

Turkeys that fly up to roost do it in timber that is substantially bigger than twenty-five-year-old slash. In an adjoining county to Clarke, I have measured a loblolly that was 14 inches in diameter at 114 feet. Add another 20 feet for the height of the top, and a turkey roosted in such a specimen is 45 yards off the ground when he is sitting still; and, unless you are directly under the tree in which he is roosted, is stationary — but out of range.

There are more trees with total heights of 130 feet than you would expect there to be — enough to get turkeys well off the ground.

There are ridges to walk, some of them with 70 and 80 percent slopes to their sides, that afford you a marvelous opportunity to walk along the crest, see 250 yards on either side, and hear across twice that distance in both directions.

And, best of all, the roll of the land gives you acres and acres of dead space, places in defilade on the other side of hills, areas you can listen in before you have to look at them. Better yet, when they do come under your observation, you can do your observing an inch at a time.

The trouble with line of sight is that the sight part runs in both directions.

You hear suspicious noises in the leaves on the other side of a thicket just in front of you, and you are left with a single choice. You have to stop and stand motionless until the noise dies away, or identifies itself to you in some positive manner, or whatever it is making the noise comes close enough for you to pick out, through the bushes, whether it is deer or chipmunk, armadillo or thrasher, turkey or Carolina wren.

When it does come in sight, the range is sometimes 15 yards.

In flat country, walk down any woods road that has a green patch planted at the end of it, and when you round the final bend and are able to see into the patch, anything in the patch is equally as able to see out. You frequently get a fine view of the back end of a turkey gobbler going out the other end of the patch at a dead run; or worse, one you never do see at all steps out of the field and walks off as soon as he sees you. The worst mistakes of all are the ones you commit not knowing you did them, when unconscious stupidity drops a hammer you didn't even know was poised to fall.

Put some roll in the ground, the more abrupt the better, and you put a lot of weight back on your end of the scales.

Hearing suspicious noises in a hollow on either side of your ridge lets you kneel down and creep over to the side and just put one eye over to look. Or, if the noises move off parallel to the ridge, you can get on the other side, run far enough to get past the sounds, and then come back just over the top and hide, to wait for them to catch up to you.

If the green patch is uphill, you can ease up the road a step at a time. Every step adds an additional 10-yard strip completely across the patch to your view. Do it slowly enough, and there is at least an even chance you might see what is in the patch before it sees you.

Hilly country lets you see things first sometimes. Best of all, it often gives you options.

It gave me one that first Friday afternoon, and the fact that I couldn't take advantage of the gift was nobody's fault but mine.

There was a logging road in reasonably good shape going west along the crest of a long ridge. The road ran generally uphill. Just at the point where a branch road took off due north, the ground pitched up sharply. The fork was at the southeast corner of two long Bahia grass patches that joined at the fork.

Neither grass patch was more than 30 yards wide. The one continuing west along the side of the road was perhaps 200 yards long, and the one going north narrowed down to about 10 yards wide and finally pinched out at a clump of eighty-year-old longleaf nearly 300 yards away.

I turned north at the fork, went about 50 yards along the road on the edge of the right-hand hollow. Around the curve, almost at the clump of pine at the end of the patch, was a turkey gobbler out in the grass, picking along the edge of the road, going in the same direction as I was.

He was a dandy, and he was by himself.

When he moved straight away, I couldn't see it; but when he moved a little to the right or left, I could see his beard dragging on the ground as he reached down to peck.

The grass was no higher than your lawn just after you cut it, and I had walked far enough around the curve to be neatly nailed; so I stopped, stayed absolutely motionless in the middle of the road, and tried to imitate a pine snag that had been dead since Calvin Coolidge was president.

Sometimes you can get away with it, and this was one of the times. I had a face net down, had gloves on, had been moving slowly, and just by chance, he had had his back turned and his attention directed toward something else when I came around the bend.

In front of him was a tiny fold in the ground. Even though I couldn't see into the bottom of it, it looked deep enough to hide him as he picked his way north. He came to it, began to go down the little slope, and as soon as his head disappeared, I broke for the side of the road and sat down as quickly as I got there.

If you had taken a week to look for it, you couldn't have found a more inferior place to sit down. For a backrest there was a 2-inch hickory with a branch stub sticking out right at the fifth vertebra down from your neck. For front cover, a scrawny crataegus bush that was too close to the hickory to be clear of the gun barrel, and the slope of the ground between the hickory and the crataegus was steep enough to have you sitting in the position that jockeys call acey-ducey, one leg a foot below the other in the stirrups.

There was no fox inside my tunic, gnawing at my vitals, like the one under the cloak of the apocryphal Spartan in the storybooks; but taken as a whole, the lack of this fox was the only good thing you could say about the setup.

There was no reason to think the turkey would turn and come back at my yelp, but there was no reason to think he would not, either. To spend time scrambling up and down the hill looking for a good place to sit was stupid, because it was conceivable he would turn around and come back before I could yelp and catch me in mid-scramble. To stay where I was, cocked sideways and uncomfortable, was a paragraph and a half beyond hopeless.

Down and hopeless, hoping to make things no worse than they already were, I got the call out of my top pocket and in my mouth and yelped one time. Cramped and awkward as the position was, I was going to have to depend upon a combination of dumb luck and total immobility to handle him if he came up.

Dumb luck and total immobility are a pair of extremely frail reeds to lean on in such situations. Frail to the point of impossibility.

You kill old turkeys like this one, at 4:30 in the afternoon, only under very special circumstances.

You might if they have had hens in the morning and the harem has drifted off to lay eggs, but it was too early in the season for that.

You might if you have stumbled over one that has not yet collected his entourage and established a lek.

You might if you have simply decided to put in the afternoon brooding over a green field or a chufa patch, and a turkey wandered into it on his way to visit friends in the next township.

Or you might if God, personally, had voted to make you Soldier of the Month and had decided to give you an 18-pound reward for your performance.

I had drawn none of these cards.

All I had really drawn was a location.

The location of a turkey gobbler, by himself, an hour and a half before roosting time, that didn't know I was there, and that wouldn't find out, unless I did something stupid, like Charlie Brown trying to steal home.

I toughed it out for thirty minutes. He didn't make a sound, he didn't appear again out in the Bahia grass, and he never showed up in the woods on my side of the slope.

Thirty yards or so in front of me was a decent-looking spot. There was an oak to lean against, the ground in front of the oak was flat, and there were some bushes growing between me and the new place that I could cut off on the way to the tree to help with the blind.

I did the crawling, and interim clipping and sitting back down in comfort, without running off anything that I was aware of, which is, in itself, no guarantee.

Nothing gave an alarm putt and ran off, nothing flew out over the hollow, nothing dashed off in terror. On the other hand, there was no guarantee that he had not been standing on the slope 150 yards away, judging the grade and quality of the crawl critically, and walking away firmly after having awarded it a low D-minus.

When you move in a situation like this, you are exchanging surety for comfort. Not the surety of killing the turkey, but the surety of not running him off.

I had known where he was, known he was not scared, known he was in earshot of my yelping, and known he was an hour and a half from the roost. The possibilities at that point were all in my favor, or as close as they ever get.

Maybe he hung around that field till roost time. Maybe he roosted in the hollow east of the grass patch. Maybe he walked back along the same road I had walked in on to roost south of the fork. Maybe he would stand around out there and drum, and then walk over to where he heard the yelping come from — I knew he had heard it. Maybe another turkey, one I had no idea was in the world, had heard the yelping and was on his way to investigate.

The way to take advantage of any of these possibilities, if any of them exists at all, is to keep still and wait until the situation develops.

It is possible that moving 30 yards to ease your back and put a cushion under your wrinkled old ass won't eliminate a single one of them, but the guarantee is gone. Move, and you may have sold the guarantee for comfort.

For whatever reason, I sat there in the new place till flying-up time and heard nothing. On the way back, I stopped from time to time and gobbled, hoping to make one gobble from the roost, one I hadn't heard fly up. By the time I got back to the truck, I had heard nothing but owls, it was nearly dark, and, although I didn't know it yet, I had just seen the only turkey I was going to get a look at in three days.

The next morning I stopped on the same road a quarter-mile past the place where I had last seen yesterday's gobbler disappear into the little fold in the grass patch, and I got there in the dark,too.

I heard three turkeys in three different directions, all three close enough to start to. All three gobbled twice, at an interval sufficient to get me going in that direction at almost a trot. And all three stopped at least two gobbles short of the amount of gobbling it would have taken me to get there and get set up.

I yelped, and prowled roads and hawked, and hooted, and cawed, and cut, and even used my patented secret pileated-wood-pecker call — known only to me and several thousand other people — all of us busily proving that P. T. Barnum was right. Most of us, after being born at the rate of one every minute, really do stay that way for the rest of our lives.

The sun shone, the birds sang, gentle breezes caressed the cheeks of poets and danced the hell out of daffodils, and the peace and tranquility of the morning was undisturbed by any rude turkey noises at all.

That afternoon, an hour and a half earlier than I had been the previous day, I walked a half-mile past the scene of yesterday's encounter and found a 5-acre green patch on the side of the road. Halfway between yesterday's Bahia patch and the clover field there was a chufa patch with a moderate amount of scratching in it and, across its upper side, enough dusting places to make you think there had been a mortar barrage.

I don't want to sound like one of those trout fishermen who imply that if you don't catch him on a barbless size 22 Quill Gordon, fished dry, you might just as well use dynamite, but I ain't really into sitting over chufa patches.

It is neither illegal nor fattening but in the English novels it is the point where the author used to write in the three dots.

The hero and the girl go into the mountains together and get caught in one hell of a storm. In the middle of the storm, they stumble across a cozy cabin. They go into the cabin and you suspect they do what people normally do in such circumstances, but the author was too cultivated to write about it.

He just wrote: "The door shut" and added ". . ."

There are a lot of turkeys killed this way, and I don't mean written to death in mountain cabins. If a man is patient, and will spend afternoons over a chufa patch or a green field, and spend enough of them, he will kill some turkeys every year. Periodically, I will get a letter from a man who tells me he has been hunting for five or six years and has killed several turkeys. But he has had so much more luck in the afternoon than he has had in the morning that he has about abandoned mornings altogether and intends to specialize in afternoon hunts.

When you get a letter like this, you know you are dealing with a man who has just gotten to the devious stage. The devious stage is populated by those who sit over chufa patches or green fields, and every twenty minutes or so, cluck once or twice.

It doesn't hurt a thing, it conceivably could attract a turkey that happened to be 80 yards away at the time you clucked. But it does one thing for sure.

Nobody is there but you, there are no other witnesses, you are calling — a cluck every twenty minutes technically qualifies as calling — and if the turkey that was coming to the patch anyhow, comes up, you can collect him.

You have therefore qualified, technically, to be able to say, "I called him up," and if you choose to embellish the story with the difficulties you had in talking him away from his three hen companions, two of whom were good looking, there is nobody to stand there clearing his throat and casting his eyes heavenward while you do it.

I didn't sit over the chufa patch. I spent part of the afternoon between the chufa patch and the green field, part of it on some roads that ran on top of some long ridges north of the green field, and finished, at roosting time, near where I had gotten into the middle of all the phantom gobbling early that morning.

On my way back to the truck at dusk, I looked in on the chufa patch. There had been an additional mortar barrage sometime during the afternoon and there were fresh gobbler droppings in the road right on the edge of the patch.

The next morning, the last of my visit, I stood on the south end of the green field and heard a single turkey gobble away off to the east. He gobbled twice and would have been easy enough to go to if you could do the 880 in 1:50, flat, carrying a shotgun.

Those of us who can't make that kind of time get in the truck and go home.

On the way to the lodge, and on the drive home, I began to get one of those feelings in the back of my neck.

Leaving out the trip to Florida, and even there, as a matter of fact, I had been around a lot of turkeys, and had heard very, very little.

Not seeing much is of little concern. This occupation is

carried on principally by ear, not by eye; and whether you can get to them or not, you ought to hear something.

We were not hearing what we ought to hear.

Back when I used to spend most Saturdays looking at what were called "action epics," there were some dependable ground rules, and Hollywood was very good at giving early notice.

If, for instance, fairly early in the movie — say, the first fifteen minutes — somebody coughed, that was the indicator. You knew for a certainty he was not going to be around for the ticker tape parade and the brass band at the finale.

You needed to spend no time getting to like him. He was marked from then on. The bony hand was right behind his shoulder, and it was simply a matter of time till the hammer fell.

We had a lot of season left, a lot more opportunities in a lot more places, and a pile of innings yet to come.

But way back in the right-hand corner of the cab, very faintly but unmistakably plain, I thought I heard somebody coughing.

6

HOME FIELD

On March 27, back from Paynes Prairie, back from Clarke County, and with the season seven days old, I finally made it to the home field.

The home ground is anywhere in the southwestern part of Alabama, the three- or four-county area I was born in, started off in, and the place I hunt in all the time.

The home field is the native hearth, the place you really know.

This business of knowing the native hearth is worth a little bit of explanation.

All hunters will say they know the lands they hunt or lease unless they have access to a tremendous acreage, or unless they are very unusual individuals. This really means only that they know the road net. They only think they know the rest.

Sometimes this conviction that they know the land can lead them into spectacular error.

I remember an instance some thirty years ago, when I was part of the search party looking for a small aircraft that had gone down. The location was somewhere above the Alabama River cutoff, between the rivers, but supposedly south of Thomasville, Alabama, a trifling area of some 750,000 acres.

One of the people who met us at the airport was the president of one of the hunting clubs in the area, a group that leased about 3,000 acres, who informed us that he knew that swamp like the palm of his hand — he had hunted it since he was a boy — and could take us anywhere we wanted to go.

I have met rather a lot of these palm-of-the-hand woodsmen over the years, but this specimen absolutely won the prize for confidence. Most of them don't go quite that far. Most of them claim an intimate knowledge of only 15,000 acres or so. This particular Indian guide, it turned out, could barely find the river and finally had the grace to sit in the back of the boat and shut up.

An acre of land is a football field, less the end zones, cut off at the 9-yard line on one end. Put trees and bushes in such an area and it becomes pretty big indeed. A square with 440 yards to the side, a quarter of a mile, contains 40 acres. A square 1 mile on a side has 640 acres. One thousand acres is a hell of a big place.

There is really only one way to have an intimate knowledge of a tract of land. You can't do it by driving over it, you can't gain the knowledge by running the lines and corners, you can't even get it by cruising the timber.

You have to mark the timber by yourself — all of it.

A man who marks the timber on a tract of land walks to every tree. He may not mark the tree for cutting, he may decide it needs to be left; but to make up his mind whether to cut it or leave it, he has to walk up to it, and after he gets there, he usually has to look at it from more than one side.

If he marks it in company with another timber marker, and if the two of them work in adjoining drifts, he is nearly as knowledgeable, though not quite. If it is a small area, and he has hunted in it or walked through it on a regular basis, over a period of years and in a variety of seasons, he knows enough to operate in it. But there are still surprises.

What he has, after several years of doing this, is an intimate knowledge of various parts; a kind of known mosaic, with areas of surprises in between, like the parts of a jigsaw puzzle he has not fitted together yet.

I have hunted the home field regularly, spring and fall, for thirty years, but I have never marked it. This means there are these 5,000 acres that I know moderately well.

Parts of it I know very well, but I can still walk up to a slough, look across it, and say, "Well, I'll be damned." Because the area across the slough is familiar, but turns out to be not in the place I thought it was.

I know the acre, but it is not in the place I thought I left it. Someone has moved it a half-mile south since last year.

You can be as good as you will let yourself believe you are with land, but there is still room for confusion.

Forty years ago, I worked with a man whose recall of specific tracts of timber had to be seen to be believed.

It was the custom then — and still is — to furnish timber-marking help for any of the log suppliers on timber he had bought from an individual owner. My friend did such marking at least once a week. Frequently, you could overhear one side of conversations on the office phone, or be present at a face-to-face confrontation, where the log supplier in question said that the tract was not going to cut out the volume supposed to have been marked, sometimes as long as six months ago.

This individual marker would begin a series of questions, like "Have you crossed the creek behind the old school site yet?" Or "How about that long ridge going west from the old cemetery?" Or "Did you cross the Fox place and get everything that is cut off between the creek and the land line?"

No reference to a map or to notes, simply pulling out the recollection of 200 acres marked six months ago, from the middle of hundreds of acres of timber marked both before and after the fact, and being right most of the time. He had a case of total recall that was almost eerie.

Or the old logging superintendent who helped me with the bridge survey.

I had been informed, by telephone, that my request for $5,000, to buy treated timbers for stream crossings on log roads, would be approved if I could tell the caller the scope of the whole program: how many bridges we had, how much treated timber we would need, and how long it would take to replace all the logging bridges on the whole tract, some 52,000 acres.

Stream crossings in the flatwoods are commonly made by cutting down the six nearest trees, cabling them into two spans of three logs each, and bridging the creek with three logs under each tire track. When they get old, they rot and fall to pieces; and the next time somebody logs in there, he makes a new bridge.

Headquarters said they needed these answers before the budget numbers went north next Wednesday, and this was Friday afternoon.

Normally, things like this don't really bother anybody. Higher headquarters have always specialized in preposterous requests for impossibly detailed information in laughably unrealistic time frames. I think they do it to establish an intellectual ascendancy over the lower ranks. Since everybody knows these requests are stupid, you simply think up a reasonable piece of fiction and send it up. They never know the difference because they never intended to use the information anyway.

Before I could concoct my estimate, the old man said, "Tom, let me sit here for about thirty minutes, and I may be able to come up with something closer than you can guess."

He was forty years my senior, had been on the land since 1903, and whatever guess he could come up with was going to be better than mine, even if he stirred old sheep guts with a stick and based his judgment on the subsequent pattern. So I agreed.

He pulled his hat down over his eyes — he wore it in-the-office all the time, to show he wasn't an office type — got his pipe going good, swiveled his chair around, put his feet up on the windowsill, and communed with Unknown Gods, turning back to make a note from time to time.

Thirty minutes later, he said, "Tom, we got eighty-three bridges and it will take just under a half-million feet of treated timbers to replace them all. Figure on the road crew doing it in about five years."

I turned his numbers in, and the next week, on no particular schedule, we had people begin to make a count as they went about other things. We finished the survey in a month and a half.

He was exactly right on the number of bridges, and his 500,000-foot estimate on the timbers was just 4,000 feet low.

He said their footage number was wrong. Somebody in the survey had made a mistake.

People like these two guys know land. The rest of us just fool around with it a little.

But even these two could get confused. I have seen the both of them, while not exactly lost, get pretty thoroughly confused and come out of the woods in surprising places.

Land and timber surprise you all the time, like the surprise I got, my first afternoon back on the home field.

The river was gone. The paper showed the Alabama to be at 17-1/2 feet at Claiborne and the Mobile just under 7 feet at Bucks. The entire swamp was open, no backwater anywhere but in the sloughs, which were emptying out fast, and there were two visible rings left on trees by the backwater.

At about 6-1/2 feet, there was a distinct yellow ring of pollen about an inch wide. It was almost as plain as if it had been painted, though painted with an inferior grade of pale yellow paint with too much thinner in it.

At about 18 inches, there was a 1/2-inch ring of oak catkins stuck to the trunks of everything. The water had evidently been at the higher level when the oaks were in pollen, and the catkins — the male flowers — had fallen off the trees and had been in the water long enough at the 18-inch level to make the lower ring.

There was a cool northwest wind at 4:00 a.m. and a pronounced thunderstorm way south of me at daylight.

I heard a little gobbling. Since being back home, I had spent a good deal of time on the telephone, and the reports of little to no gobbling were beginning to come in from all sides.

The swamp was open, the mosquitoes had not yet attained mean annual increment, though you could see it coming, and we were, as yet, not into the yellow-top season.

There was very little sign in the pine uplands. It appeared that turkeys were still in the swamp and engaged in beachcombing. They had followed the backwater as it receded, the ones that spent two weeks in trees were down, everything was still in flux, and some of us still thought we were between the two peaks of gobbling. We had missed the first one because the spring had been so early and had not yet come to the second.

The morning of March 30 was a bird walk; without turkeys, really, because some of the gobbling was so far off it was at least pseudo-imaginary, but with almost everything else. Not the least was an entire drove of hummingbirds on a patch of red buckeye at the edge of the swamp.

We never see hummingbirds around the feeder until late in June, though they come through in late March and early April. In the last week of October, just about the time the males migrate south, there will often be a half-dozen around the feeder on the back deck. If there was one in this patch of buckeye there were fifteen. They ain't easy to count, but, in my opinion, fifteen hummingbirds constitute a drove. There really ought to be some descriptive group term for them other than "drove." Something like "wisps" of snipe or "exaltations" of larks; but if there is one, I am unaware of it.

Although I did not get to work a turkey, after I had given up and was simply prowling, I got surprised by a stump. Nothing out of the ordinary as to species, but distinctly out of the ordinary as to location.

Most hardwood trees can withstand a degree of flooding and some period of standing water. Yellow poplar is the exception in that it cannot, which is why you find no yellow poplar in the river swamp. Water tupelo and cypress are on the wet end of the acceptability curve, and beech and cherry bark oak on the dry end. Pine is off by itself. Pine can hardly take water at all.

As you get 75 miles off the coast, you begin to see occasional spruce pines in the swamp, generally on the natural levee near the river. But as a general empirical statement, if it floods and water stands on it, it is a hardwood site, and you couldn't grow pine on it even if you tried.

So all over the lower swamp there are old stumps — the very oldest, cypress, because of its resistance to rot — but invariably hardwood, because they are in river bottoms.

One of the oldest criminal traditions in the United States is timber theft. From the days before the American Revolution, when the British navy marked white pine in New England with the king's arrow, to reserve that tree for masts and spars, timber thieves have been among us. In point of fact, some of the oldest fortunes in the United States came originally from stolen trees.

We had no white pine in south Alabama, but we did have cypress; and cypress, in addition to all its other splendid characteristics, like straight grain and resistance to rot, had one premier quality.

It was remarkably easy to transport after you stole it.

Stealing trees is not as easy as stealing apples, for instance. You shake the tree, put the fallen apples in your pockets, and walk off. Don't get too greedy and take too many; and, except for lumpy pockets, you don't really call too much attention to yourself as you go.

A 30-inch white pine, with four logs in it, weighs about 8 tons. After you cut it down and work it into logs, you have to move it, and you have to have something substantial to move it with. Oxen, mule teams, railroads, trucks, are all big and noisy and expensive and hard as hell to hide.

Pick a cypress that size or bigger, girdle it with an ax two years before you need to move it, and three things happen. It loses half the weight it had when green, the heartwood is so rot resistant that two years on the stump does nothing to hurt it, and when the yearly floods come and you cut it down, it floats. This last is important, because all green hardwood, except ash, sinks like stone. It has to dry out some before it will float.

You make a little noise with your ax when you girdle the tree, and you make a little more when you cut it down two years later, but it floats in absolute silence. You have to sort of herd it along with your boat, and the place you intend to take it has to be downstream; but the whole operation is quiet, efficient, effective, and most economical in terms of capital requirements and fuel consumption. It is truly an elegant solution.

Scattered all through the swamp are cypress stumps, many of them 10 feet high. Cutting them when the swamp was flooded got you above the butt swell, and it was easier to go and come in the swamp by boat — floating beats walking. From the number of stumps you find, it is evident that many of our ancestors took an opportunity to borrow some of the government's cypress — there clearly was plenty — and since there was such an abundance, it would have been superfluous to bother anybody by talking about it.

That first afternoon, prowling around between the morning and the afternoon hunt, I dropped down off a mixed pine-and-hard-wood ridge and went nearly 150 yards into the swamp.

Right where I stopped there was a medium-sized stump, about head high, with a jagged top. Some of these older stumps are so old that the top is no longer flat, and some come from trees blown down or broken off. This one had a sharp, jagged point, like a stalagmite, was right by my hand, and I absentmindedly pushed on the point to break it off.

It was absolutely solid. Old cypress, worn down this thin, is not supposed to be very solid, so I took hold of the point and leaned back. It broke off below my hand down where it was nearly an inch thick. As soon as the piece broke off, I smelled it.

It was pine. Not only was it pine, it was pure, fat lightwood.

I could hardly have been more surprised if it had been redwood. Pine cannot grow in swamps like this. The area was pure river bottom, had the pollen ring from the last high water up at the 6-foot level, just like everything else from here to the bank of the river itself, and, with very rare exceptions, stayed 6 feet under water from the middle of December till the middle of April every single year with very rare exceptions.

There were more than a dozen of these stumps, scattered irregularly across an acre or so. Reconstructing the size of the tree from the arc of the fat stump left and adding in a normal amount for sapwood and bark, the biggest one of them had been a 30-inch tree.

I went back to the truck, picked up a half-sized bow saw I carry to cut limbs out of the road, came back to the stump, and cut off part of it. It is on the desk before me as I write this.

It is fat lightwood, as heavy and full of pitch as any pine stump anywhere in Alabama. If you showed it to me and told me it came from the river swamp, I would not believe a single syllable.

But it did.

I can take you back to the stump and show you where I cut it by fitting the cut-off piece back on the stump left in the woods.

It almost has to be loblolly or slash. The hill adjoining that area of swamp where I found it is a mixed stand of loblolly and hardwood, eighty years old, with much more hardwood than pine. There is no pith in the piece I have, nor in any of the stumps I found, so I cannot say it was longleaf. The characteristics of the rings mitigate against spruce. I think it is loblolly, but then, what the hell do I know. I didn't think it could have been there in the first place at all.

Neither loblolly nor slash produces any substantial amount of heartwood until it gets into the 100- to 125-year age class. For heart-wood to have been formed as far out from the center as it is in this specimen, the tree had to have been in the 200-year class when it died.

Loblolly seedlings cannot withstand flooding for very long. Older trees can take it for a while, and the older the tree the longer it can take it, until the tree becomes overmature and has been weakened by heart rot.

There must have been a period when there was a drought of sufficient severity to allow loblolly seedlings to come into this area, and the drought had to be sufficient length to allow the trees to reach at least pole size before normal weather patterns came back. In addition, the area had to be largely open ground at the time of germination because while loblolly might germinate under severe hardwood shade, it cannot survive there.

In the thirty years I have hunted this tract, I must have gone through this area two hundred times. The pine-hardwood ridge at the edge of the swamp is a great place to listen from. From there you can hear turkeys gobble from the north fence to Blue Boat Lake, and I have spent enough time on that ridge, listening, to qualify to vote in the precinct.

These stumps never came to my attention before because they are off site, are not supposed to be down there in the swamp, and, consequently, are invisible.

I have some evidence that suggests when they seeded in and when they died.

I have a three-legged table, made from a wheel cut off the butt log of an old-growth longleaf, that was cut in Conecuh County, 90 miles east of here, in 1959. The tree was 183 years old when cut, and somewhere around 1900, allowing five years for the tree to get out of the grass stage, there is a distinct pattern.

There is a wide growth ring, then two narrow ones, another wide, two very narrows, and another wide. There is no other comparable pattern all the way back to 1776, the year the tree seeded in. There has been no comparable pattern seen on other logs in the thirty-six years since 1959.

There is a comparable pattern of wide, narrow, narrow, wide, narrow, narrow, wide, in the sawn-off specimen here on the desk.

Weather records show considerable variation in rainfall patterns at Mobile at the turn of the century, with the highest ever recorded — 91 inches — in 1900, and the second-lowest — 39 inches — in 1904.

If you assign the year 1900 to the pattern in the sample, to match the pattern in the table, you conclude that this stump seeded in around 1780 and died about 1950.

There is no evidence of drought/rain in the 1770-to-1800 time frame — weather records at Mobile are not available before 1887 — but the tree stump is there, is fat lightwood, and could not have produced that much heartwood until it was nearly two centuries old.

It is anybody's guess as to what cleared the land. There was farming in the area before 1775, but generally only right on the riverbanks.

There have been climatic changes other than those associated with the glaciers, and some of them have been pronounced enough to do some things to vegetation that look strange. Something did away with the canes that Bartram saw; ". . . canes *(Arundo gigantea) grow* here thirty or forty feet high, and as thick as a man's arm, or three or four inches in diameter; I suppose one joint of some of them would contain above a quart of water. . . ." Something put 200-year-old loblolly in the river swamp and took it out again.

It is my position that there have been moderate climatic changes between glaciers, and that there was one in the late eighteenth century that was severe enough to culminate in the fat pine stumps in the swamp that surprised me so sharply last March.

I find this theory to be reasonable, but no one else has any obligation to follow my rationale.

You may be the most confirmed finger crosser of them all, and believe that there was a species of loblolly pine, *Pinus taeda* var. *bottomlandicus,* that throve in river swamps and is now extinct. If so, feel free. Here, lately, people have gotten their names in the paper and their opinions before the American Botanical Society on evidence not much better than that.

If you got as far as Caesar's *Gallic Wars* in third-year Latin, then you know enough Latin to be able to write up the botanical term without misspelling too many of the words. Write it up just right, be persistent enough, and you may be able to get it named after you — "var. *bottomlandicus*" whatever. Then you and Mrs. Mary G. Henry can go in the book together.

I will be happy to show you the stumps.

7

JACKPOT

On Friday morning, March 31, there was a driving rain at 4:00 a.m. The weather station the night before had shown a line of thunderstorms coming out of Louisiana, and there were wind gusts of 30 miles an hour. I looked out the window and went back to bed.

You never abandon a morning like this without a serious attack of conscience, although the attack is nothing like what it used to be back in the bad old days.

When the season started on March 20 and ended on April 15, as it did for years, and you came to the last of March, you were nearly halfway through. There were twelve days down and fifteen to go.

Wasting a morning for something so unimportant as sleep will always be sinful. It just used to appear infinitely more sinful when you used up one of the fifteen days you had left, rather than one of the thirty.

You generally sin in this fashion on the basis of weather; so if you go back to bed and it rains like hell, and is still raining when you do get up, there is the distinct feeling that you got away with one. You sinned, but the recording angel was taking the afternoon off, and there was nobody there to write it down.

If you get up later, to no rain and a bright sun, it makes things worse. The fact that up in the woods, where the turkeys are, it may or may not be sunny, is immaterial. Your intellect may tell you that what is happening just outside the window doesn't count. The difficulty lies in convincing your gut.

Gut feeling is what points out to us that we are not quite as sophisticated as we think we are. Let me lay a "for instance" on you to demonstrate.

Some years ago, I was present when a gun section in a self-propelled 155mm battery dropped a fused projectile while lifting it from the floor of the carrier up to the loading tray. A 155mm projectile weighs 96 pounds, fused. The shell hit nose down but at an angle, and the fuse broke but did not come completely off and remained, still screwed down into the projectile, but broken above the screws and cocked sideways at something like a 40-degree angle.

Remembering pressing business they had neglected to attend to back around the motor park, the gun section came out of the M-109 like angry hornets leaving the nest. We cleared everybody else out of the way, and two of us went into the tracked carrier to remove the fuse.

The thing was absolutely safe. Before such a fuse can be activated, the projectile must be fired, inertia must move a sliding block in a groove inside the fuse back out of the way, and the projectile must rotate a sufficient number of times for centrifugal force to move a blocking pin out of the path so that the explosion of the fulminate of mercury can get to the TNT after the projectile impacts.

Every bit of this is assimilated into your intellect in the first course of Basic Artillery Ammunition 101.

Absolutely none of it penetrates to the gut.

Here were two people, kneeling on both sides of 96-pound projectile, one holding it upright while the other was using a hammer and a wrench, trying to get the bottom half of the fuse out of the cavity, struggling with their intellects.

It was astonishing to feel the way the hairs on the back of your neck stood up while you tapped on the fuse wrench with a hammer, and stood a little higher with each successive tap.

We got it out and, since I am writing this after the fact, nobody got blown away. There was never the slightest chance that anybody would, but it gives you a real appreciation of why practitioners of voodoo fear Baron Samedi. They are listening to their gut.

In a perfect world, populated by perfect people, you would get up and go hunt every morning, regardless. And regardless means exactly what its definition says it means.

You would get wet more often. You would spend mornings in the woods knowing that every turkey in the county was safely aloft in his roost tree and was not coming down till the rain stopped, and that the stupidest attendee at the whole affair was the one standing under the tree. But your gut would be at ease.

In my next reincarnation, I am going to reform. I am going to get up and go every time.

The morning of Saturday, April 1, I got my lazy butt out of bed at the proper time, went to the woods, and found the mother lode.

I stopped to listen at daylight, on the ridge above the magic stumps, and between then and 10:00 a.m., when I finally left the woods, had found fifteen separate turkeys, had a solid fix on all fifteen locations, and a known route to all of them. On the next morning, on Sunday, April 2, I found an additional eight. This amounts to twenty-three confirmed locations in two days, enough to constitute two seasons' work.

There was a solid gobble at daylight on Saturday, due west of the ridge and probably on that long gum-cypress pond that begins a half-mile south of the sound of the gobble and runs north into Pine Log Creek.

I went off into the swamp at a walk nearly fast enough to be a trot, went 300 yards, and stopped to listen for some more help.

It is flat as a table in there. There is absolutely no understory, but there is, as absolutely, no roll to the ground, either. When you step down into the swamp, you are on the 10-foot contour line.

Three-quarters of a mile northwest, the same contour line bends around and you cross it again, and there has been no intervening line in between the two points. The operative word is flat, and because it is, and because of the lack of understory, going to a gobbling turkey is a knee slapper when it comes to direction. The thorn on the rose is distance, and the ground is so open that it is easy to get too close.

Unless you were right up against him the first time he did it, you need at least two more gobbles, and maybe three.

What I got was nothing. He was out there in front of me, maybe close enough to call to, but probably not. In the absence of any other indication, there was nothing to do but wait him out.

I stood and waited, and twitched and waited, and squirmed and waited, and after a while, just waited.

Away off to the northwest, almost out of hearing, but definitely there, a turkey gobbled three or four times. This could not have been the one I started to. He had to be all the way up in Hogan's Bend. I hung around another fifteen minutes and then sat down, tried to act as if there was a turkey 300 yards away, occupied the position as if I intended to stay there until 11:30, and yelped exactly as I would have if I were positive he had just flown down.

There is a technical name for this maneuver: it is called playing out the string. It has the same feeling of hopeless rage you get when you pop up to the second baseman with the bases loaded. You have to run it out and you do, but you wish you had another leg that you could be using to kick your own ass with while you ran. Run them out for three years religiously, and nothing happens. Don't do it once — just once — and the infielder drops the ball and then picks it up and throws to first base, where you ought to be standing, but ain't, and you end the inning.

I ran it out for three-quarters of an hour, and then got up and instead of going straight back out of the swamp the way I had come in, did a long circle that would take me along the south bank of Pine Log Creek, to see what things looked like up there, and to stop and cut and caw and hoot along the way, trying to make one gobble on the ground.

The first turkey flushed out of a tree before I had gone 200 yards. He was not the turkey I had gone to because his direction was too much at variance with the direction I had first taken. But he was close enough to have been partly disturbed while I waited, and then set up. Too far away to fly, but near enough to neither gobble on his own nor answer any of my yelps.

I ran the second one out of his tree just before I got back to the hill. What had kept him up there that long was another of those mysteries, of constantly increasing number, like the McDonald's signs that used to tell how many billions of hamburgers had been sold.

Both these turkeys were gobblers, or pterodactyls — I

never heard a pterodactyl fly out of a tree before, so I can't be positive — but way too big to be hens. The second one sounded as if he took 20 pounds of leaves and twigs off the top of the tree when he left.

These things happen. They are not worth getting ulcers over, or even going home and taking it out on the wife and kids. And they have a good side. I now had the location of four turkeys, two by sound and two by sight, all gobblers, none of them across geographical boundaries or impossible sloughs, and all of which would, presumably, gobble properly later on.

If you ain't been whipped worse than this, then you ain't been around long enough for your opinions to matter.

In my opinion, those states that forbid afternoon hunting make a mistake. In doing so, they cater to the inherent laziness of most hunters and create the afternoon drive-around.

People will conclude that since we can't hunt, if we stay here at the camp house until time to roost something, we will either play poker and lose money, or drink too much. If there is a place to bream-fish, okay; but if not, let's go drive around and see if we see anything.

Turkeys don't need to see people every day. Turkeys that are driven under, yelped at, flushed out of fields and green patches, and generally stirred up day after day after day, get spooky. So I don't spend a hell of a lot of time driving around to see if I see something. Early in the season, I may drive a little, and until there are some located, yes. To take a guest to a specific location to show him the land so he will know exactly where to go in the morning, yes. Wandering around in the equivalent of taking the old folks on a Sunday-afternoon drive, no.

Promulgating edicts to forbid afternoon hunting pushes people out there driving around, drinking beer and playing the radio, and making infinitely more noise and creating ten times the disturbance they would create if they were out there, dozing over a green patch, or fast asleep under a tree.

Those whom the gods would destroy, they first make stupid.

This particular Saturday, being early in the season and with very little located, circumstances turned me loose, so I spent about an hour hunting through the windshield.

I saw five gobblers, in ones and twos at various crossings and patches, and almost back at the camp house, right at the last, there was a group of six old gobblers out in the power line, on a ridge a half-mile from where I sat, spending the morning out in the sun.

At any given time, two or three of them would strut and fan their tails. They wandered back and forth across the grass under the power poles, picking occasionally and strutting occasionally. Once, all six were in a full strut at the same time.

I had them in the glasses for the better part of twenty minutes before they finally drifted away to the east and disappeared down in a little hollow that fed away from the line.

Coming all at once, as it did, such a collection of locations sets up the season for the rest of the year.

The first four were all in the swamp and were scattered fairly evenly across 500 acres. The last six had ample room north and east of where they were to establish territories and gather harems in the uplands. The middle five were reasonably along the break between swamp and hill and had room to operate in either direction.

There were really no more gaps to fill in.

On percentages, at least one or two of this multitude would turn into one of those turkeys that set up a location and stay there, turkeys that gobble a hundred and fifty times every morning of their lives and never come to anybody. They are called guest turkeys.

They are the heart and soul of every club that has a guest

program. They are always there, they gobble regularly, frequently, and loudly from the roost, and then constantly on the ground until 9:30. You couldn't run them away from their chosen territory with an armored regiment; and no man, living or dead, is going to kill one.

They will furnish excitement, purpose, and enjoyment to all races, creeds, colors, national origins, and levels of skill indiscriminately, and will fertilize the eggs of a dozen hens apiece while doing so.

You can send any guest you please, at whatever level of expertise he may enjoy, to any one of them, with the solid expectation of getting the turkey back unscathed upon the completion of his visit.

Such turkeys call to mind Frederick the Great's remark about lieutenant colonels: "There may be bad generals and bad privates. That is no matter. But there must not be bad lieutenant colonels, for they are the cornerstone of any army."

The balance of the count, scattered across a mixture of moisture conditions and timber types, was available to take people to, to get one hung up to be photographed every once in a while, and to put one in the freezer for yourself.

The next morning, Sunday, I went to the area where I had run the second of the two gobblers out of the tree the day before and heard nothing there at all.

There was one gobble on the north fence and two or three away to the south, but all these, I thought, came from one turkey. I left to go to the south end and see if I could shock one into gobbling down on the power line. After I set up, a half-dozen young gobblers fed across the power line just below me.

All in all, nearly an embarrassment of riches.

Twenty-three positive locations in a variety of areas. Old turkeys for the skillful, two-year-old turkeys for the harvest, and there, at the last, a drove of jakes working the power line to furnish amusement for the women and children.

I drove home wondering what the poor people were doing.

Take for openers May 15 as the usual day of hatching, back off twenty-five days for incubation, and it gets you to April 20. Go back another twelve days to allow time to lay eight to ten eggs, and that puts you at April 7. The weeks beginning April 9 and April 16 should be the second peak of gobbling, and the time from April 23 to April 30, the headache season.

The second peak tends to coincide with egg laying, when hens have visited the gobbler in the morning and have gone off to lay later in the day. From the second egg on, generally, they spend more and more time at the nest every day until incubation. During incubation they are on the nest most of the time.

Whether or not it offends your manhood and wounds your confidence, until incubation starts, hens go to gobblers, rather than gobblers going to hens. After incubation begins, the girls are gone. Until then, a brisk five minutes of gobbling from the roost every morning would gather anywhere from a half-dozen to a half-acre of hens under the tree. Now, twenty minutes of sustained yelling gets him nothing but a sore throat.

Within the space of a couple of days, he goes from a situation where he can't turn around for tripping over a fresh girl, to the point where everybody has a headache.

If it ever gets close to easy, it gets there during the headache season.

With the calm confidence of the truly rich, the ingrained arrogance that comes from the solid knowledge that probably no man in the United States that morning had more turkeys located than I did, and with both the second peak of gobbling and the headache season before me, I took the next two days off.

The first morning I had something pressing to do upstate and couldn't do both. The second morning, simply to demonstrate again that he really is on the side of the big battalions, God let it rain even after I had decided to sleep in anyway.

The morning of April 5, there was a sky full of stars at 4:45, and by daylight there was a shut-down fog in the woods.

I have never heard turkeys gobble much in the fog. They gobble a lot in the rain, and a hell of a lot in answer to thunder, but very little in fog. It is probably a combination of two things. It is likely that they gobble somewhat less for openers. Also, sounds travel so poorly in a dense fog that you hear only part of those that do.

At 8:30, with the fog at an intensity that made you expect to see two guys in fore-and-aft hats and tweeds talking about the "footprints of a gigantic hound," I left the river swamp, drove partway back to the camp house, parked, and was walking down the main road to the point where it crossed the first power line.

About 100 yards from the crossing, I got into the left-hand ditch and began to move one step at a time with the intent of getting within 20 yards of the line and trying to call up something that was out in it but had not gobbled.

The whole length of the line is planted in ryegrass and makes a green patch 2 miles long.

My forward motion may have been at the rate of 5 yards a minute, and I was within 30 yards of the edge of the clearing, when two jakes stepped out into the road from the right-hand side and nailed me.

I was between steps, had on gloves and the face net down, but was standing up, with the gun held crosswise in front and with nothing either before or behind. One of them turned back and went behind a clump of weeds on the side of the road; but the other one stood there, looking directly at me, turning his head to the side with that quizzical look they get that says: "I wonder what you are?"

Old turkeys run from wonder. Young turkeys tend to stay and puzzle things out. Consequently, many of them never last long enough to get into the old-turkey category.

I didn't want to shoot either one of these children. I wanted them to step back out of sight in the weeds and give me a chance to sit down and try to call up one of the grown folks.

They decided not to cooperate.

It is hard to be precise because there was action in and out of the road, back and forth across the road, and on both sides of the power line. But there had to have been at least eight or ten of them and they acted exactly like high-school boys hanging out on the corner by the pool hall.

They had mock fights with one another. They yelped at nothing — not loud, but at about half-volume. Turkeys raised and stretched their wings, scratched up gravel in the road, and crossed back and forth in and out of the weeds and in and out of view.

The whole thing must have lasted ten minutes. At no time were there fewer than two or three in sight. The gun got heavier and heavier, and I began to itch in more and more places.

Finally, everybody left the road going west, and I sank down gratefully, crawled to the nearest tree, sat down and put my back against it, and scratched everything I could reach.

I got the net up in front and something under me to sit on and stayed in place and yelped off and on for half an hour.

Nothing came to look. Nothing answered. Wherever the pool-hall crowd had gone, they stayed there.

I didn't. After forty minutes of nothing, my boredom threshold is crossed and I go do something else.

The next five days were all of a piece. Every morning you

heard a turkey or two or three; and every morning, every turkey gobbled two or three times.

You can't make it like that. If turkeys are going to average 2.14 gobbles or some such other silly number, the only way you are going to get to one is to be within 300 yards of him when he gobbles, or you are hunting where there is only one tree within half a mile and he can be roosting nowhere else. The trouble with this last scenario is that there would be no turkeys there to roost in the first place.

On April 11th it poured down rain all morning, and April 12th was a rerun of April 6th through 10th.

By April 12th, I had sat down to only one gobbling turkey all season. The fact that there were two there, rather than one, is not relevant. I had heard enough, for long enough, to get to exactly one gobbling turkey in twenty-two days.

Driving back home, I remember telling myself that we were now three days into my carefully calculated second peak. If what we had been hearing constituted a peak, there was damned little danger that anybody was going to suffer from altitude sickness.

There are peaks of this magnitude in the marshes at the mouth of the Mississippi River, just below Head of Passes.

We were just past the halfway point, with eighteen days left to go. There is some time left, but we are beginning to run it a little close.

Somebody might ought to point out to the U.S. cavalry that, while we were not down to the last half-bandolier of cartridges, it wouldn't hurt to put a little hurry in it. The whole thing brought up in a climate of constructive criticism, you understand.

8

THEY DON'T EVEN MAKE
THE BOXES ANYMORE

There is no intention on my part to turn this into a trip down memory lane, even though at this stage I have more left of memory than I do of lane. But there have been some pretty substantial changes in equipment and conditions since I first broke into the league almost sixty years ago.

Make no mistake about it. Every change, with virtually no exception, has been a change for the better.

The good old days are right this minute, but there is a fascination in looking back at the misery, like the fascination of remembering when there was not a single air-conditioned automobile in the state of Alabama.

In 1938, although I was not yet old enough to do it, you shaved with a Red Gillette. The Gillette company made two kinds of blades: the Red at three for ten cents, and the Blue, at three for a quarter. I knew some rich people, none of them well enough to be allowed to stand there and watch them shave, but my financial circle used the Red Gillette.

This product was still being made and sold when I came to shaving, although in the beginning it was painless.

I went into the service at the age of seventeen and was informed that membership in the armed forces of the United States carried with it the obligation of the daily shave. Being only young, rather than hopelessly stupid, I forbore to ask them exactly what it was they wanted me to shave, and scraped off the peach fuzz dutifully every morning. A couple of years later, when it really became necessary, I discovered that a Red Gillette, used for the fourth time, would make that Spartan youth who suffered the fox in silence cry when he shaved the corners of his mouth.

Another of our finest character builders was the paper shotgun shell.

Paper shotgun shells from a newly opened box, used at the rate of two boxes per sunny Saturday afternoon in a dove field, are a nonevent. High-brass fours, dropped in the inch of water that stays in the bottom of a duck boat, or loaded and reloaded through a Model 12 pump throughout a fifteen-trip turkey season, are another matter altogether. They printed the load and shot size on the top cover, under the roll crimp, so you had no trouble reading them; but after they got damp and swelled up, what you had trouble with was loading them.

Nobody every heard of camouflage clothes until after World War II, and boots ran very heavily to 16-inch knee-highs, laced all the way up.

One of the present catalogs I get from a major manufacturer (in this day and age you get a lot) is 296 pages long. Pages 1 to 123 advertise nothing but clothing, pages 123 to 180 are concerned wholly with footwear, and over 60 percent of the catalog concerns itself with dress.

Not only did we not have many turkeys in 1938, we had

a complaint similar to that of a seventeen-year-old girl just before the senior prom. We didn't have a thing to wear.

There were camouflage jackets and pants sold, principally as surplus clothing in army/navy stores after World War II, and evidently, around that time, somebody began to make and sell them, because still hanging in my closet is a pair of camouflage pants so old that they button up the fly.

It is not yet time to close the book on turkeys and color. Like everybody I know, I wear camouflage, complete with gloves and face masks. I can't tell for sure whether I believe in it or not, but I use a patented soap now sold to eliminate ultraviolet colors in the dye. Maybe it doesn't help, but it surely can't hurt. I have a half-dozen recent encounters with turkeys, so I can, without straining too hard, subscribe to the camouflage.

There is a book published by Lyons & Burford, *Illumination in the Flatwoods,* by Joe Hutto, that goes a long way toward explaining why so many turkeys were killed by people wearing faded overalls, but we will talk about this at length later on.

Surely there were diaphragm yelpers in use before World War II, but most people didn't know about them. I first saw one in about 1953 and began to use them after that. All lead and adhesive tape, all homemade and with the lead horseshoe completely exposed on one side. If you wanted to use a double, you simply sewed two of them together.

This tended to make them heavy enough to make your jaw ache, but was excellent for building up the muscles in the tongue.

It is not too much of an oversimplification to point out that World War II was somewhat of a break point. Before then people hunted in old clothes, or work clothes, or overalls. If you took things seriously, you had one of those brown canvas caps, some Filson, tin cloth, hunting pants and jacket, and your call was a slate or a box.

After the war, the general uniform was a war-surplus camouflage suit, your old combat boots rather than 16-inch lace-ups, an aspirin box with a mouth yelper in it, a pocketknife to cut bushes with, and a rolled-up copy of the *Ladies' Home Journal* to sit on. You carried your Model 12 loaded with five rounds of high-brass fours. The three-shot maximum in Alabama is mandatory only on migratory game.

Country turkey hunters were similarly equipped except they were mostly dressed in faded overalls and wore work brogans and a black felt hat.

Every once in a while you met a really old old-timer who had started hunting back when years began with 18, and who called with a wing bone.

You still stumbled upon an occasional man with a rifle. Alabama did not outlaw rifles until about 1980, and a lot of the real old-timers preferred them.

Henry E. Davis spends a lot of time talking about rifles and says that, taking everything into account, his preference would be a .22 Hornet.

Jordan, in McIlhenny, favors the .32/20 although he talks about its tending to tear up the meat.

There are states that still permit the use of the rifle, and using one would give you a tremendous advantage.

Even with iron sights, it would put the 125-yard turkey in range.

A turkey that has answered a call, or that is walking toward you looking for whoever made it, will often, except in central Florida, come into sight at 125 yards. From there, until he gets to the 40-yard marker, he might just as well be on the moon as far as effective killing range with a shotgun is concerned. A rifle would present you with 85 yards you do not now have, and furthermore, with the 85 yards where so much of the stupidity occurs.

That 85 is where you dumb things up.

You didn't bother to hide as well as you should have, and he picks you out. You try to get the gun up before his head is completely behind the tree. You figure you have enough time and distance left to be able to shift enough to ease a cramped thigh muscle. You let your nerves get the better of you and misjudge the range by 20 yards.

The closer he comes, the more vigilant he is. The bigger he looks, the more rattled you become, and the more apt you are to commit a piece of incandescent stupidity, with reason shrieking at you not to do it all the time.

This is not a campaign to resume the use of rifles in Alabama. I am like the Frenchman who saw no need at all to travel, since he was already in Paris. I don't want the last 85 yards to change because that's where all the heavy breathing goes on. But there is in inventory a turkey rifle, which was not deliberately designed as such, but just turned out that way.

Not only was it not developed as a turkey rifle, it was intended to be a people rifle — a substitute for the pistol.

The Model 1911 Cal .45 ACP holds the record as the military arm that was in active use for the longest period of time. Accepted by the U.S. army in 1911, it was the issue handgun for United States forces for seventy-five years. It has all the knockdown power you want, but is heavy, is hard to shoot well, and, like all handguns, requires the user to shoot upward of 10,000 rounds, in practice, just to become reasonably competent.

In 1941, David Williams, a designer for Winchester, came up with a gas-operated, military semiautomatic rifle using a short-stroke piston arrangement. It was not accepted for a variety of reasons, but the basic principle of the design was used when the army wanted a short carbine for issue to Armor, Artillery, and Engineer troops in lieu of the .45 pistol.

It became the U.S. Carbine Cal .30 M-l.

It is a delightful little rifle. Less than 36 inches in total length and weighing 6-1/2 pounds, it shoots a 110-grain bullet that still has 600 foot-pounds of energy at 100 yards, nearly triple that of the .32/20 that Jordan preferred.

It hasn't enough recoil to disturb a damselfly, will shoot five shot, 3-inch groups at 100 yards with military sights, and is light enough to be carried by little girls in pink Easter dresses, on their way to church.

The bullet is loaded as FMJ, does not expand, and the defect Jordan found regarding undue damage to the meat by the .32/20 would not be a factor.

The shot groups get pretty sloppy at 300 yards; but, in the woods, except very rarely, you can't see enough of a turkey to shoot him at 300 yards. If you live in a state that permits rifles, you ought to take a look at it.

When you come to the variety of auxiliary equipment that is available today, you come into another world.

Instead of keeping them all in one drawer, under the counter, the shelf space in the modern sporting-goods store that is devoted to calls alone has to be measured in feet. Nobody has to sew two lead yelpers together to make a double because there are doubles, and triples, and quads, and coarses, and fines, and on and on and on.

And nobody keeps them in aspirin boxes. In point of fact, I can't remember when it was I saw the last aspirin box — even one with aspirins in it. They have gone the way of the Red Gillette, the buttoned fly, and the paper shotgun shell, and good riddance to the lot of them.

The variation in shotgun gauges, loads, and chokes available today almost overcomplicates the selection process. You can buy virtually anything you are big enough to carry, and load it with combinations of powder and shot that would break your collarbone, if you were unintelligent enough to shoot it prone.

There is such a variety of ear-ringing and cheek-crushing loads available that there has been one unfortunate offshoot.

Some of the brethren are beginning to fool around with size 7-1/2 shot again.

Thirty years ago, there was a distinct 7-1/2-shot-size subculture. You were constantly surprised at the people who turned up with membership cards in it, sort of like finding personal friends going to chiropractors for brain tumors.

Put 4-1/2 drams of powder and 21/4 ounces of shot in one of these 31/2 inch magnums and pull the trigger, and it reminds you of a 105 howitzer firing Charge 7.

The only trouble is that noise is a valuable commodity only when it comes to calling hogs or operating boat horns. You don't kill turkeys with noise, you do it with shot.

Pack any amount of charge you please, behind any amount of shot you choose, within reason, and if you use 7-1/2 shot, you run into one of the immutable laws of physics, no matter how much noise it makes.

There are several decent studies, made mostly at the time of the steel-shot furor, that show it is necessary to have an energy of 2 foot-pounds per pellet to penetrate the skull of a turkey or the chest cavity of a large duck.

The energy level of number 7-1/2 shot falls below 2 foot-pounds per pellet at 23 yards.

If it is your normal practice to call turkeys to within 23 yards before you shoot them, you are to be commended. It is indicative of a high order in several disciplines: camouflage, woodsmanship, patience, world-class calling. I could go on to the end of the page.

But if you can do this, and I do not doubt for a minute that you can, at that range you can harvest turkeys with 3-1/4 drams of powder and an ounce of 8s, using a shell left over from last year's dove season. You don't have to have a cannon that crosses your eyes and makes your nose bleed every time you pull the trigger.

And if, God forbid, one morning you miscalculate and shoot a turkey 30 yards away, he is outside the retained-energy threshold, and you cannot kill him with 2 pounds of powder and a Luzianne Coffee can full of 7-1/2s, assuming that you can lift a weapon that holds such a charge, or that you are good enough to call him to the edge of the water where you are lying prone in your boat, behind your grandfather's ancestral punt gun.

Probably the most pronounced advances of all, in the field of equipment, are to be found in those devices that address themselves to the improvement of creature comforts. Far away at the top of this list is insect repellent.

I believe it was Tom Edison who first said that genius was 2 percent inspiration and 98 percent perspiration. Whether or not we agree with Tom's percentages, we all tend to admire perseverance. Sometimes perseverance can turn into foolish consistency, but we regularly applaud people who do not let minor difficulties interfere with the completion of their mission.

You get checked in one direction, you move immediately along direction B. B goes sour, you turn to C. You make do, improvise, use field expedients, and somehow muddle through.

You may be the best in the world at this, known across four states for your bulldog determination. The kind of hunter who puts mud on his hands if he forgets his gloves. Or hunts in his bedroom slippers if he came off without his boots. Or if he brought his gun but forgot the shells, lies down behind a log and tries to call a turkey into stabbing range of his pocketknife. You may be able to operate with nothing to sit on, nothing to wear, nothing to call with except to slap your thigh and cry, "Here, Rattler, here," or "Kitty, Kitty, Kitty."

You may be able to do all these things, and more. But we have days in Alabama, just after the backwater has left the river swamp in the spring, when the discovery that you have forgotten to bring the mosquito repellent puts you right back in the car and sends you home to Mama.

I have no idea what Daniel Boone and Davy Crockett used. Some of those homemade remedies, composed principally of citronella and other mysterious unguents, simply had a psychosomatic effect on the user, if they had any at all.

Maybe in the very old days, you simply washed so seldom that nothing could stand you, even mosquitoes.

But now we have repellents that come in little, soft squeeze bottles or wipe-on sticks that work, that are easy to use, that come in sizes that slip into the pocket so the application can be renewed from time to time, and that really and truly repel mosquitoes.

I rank this development first, above all others. Never mind sitting soft. Never mind three-reed yelpers with notches cut along one side that imitate hen turkeys in the last stages of galloping nymphomania. Never mind camouflage that can render elephants invisible. All these are pyrites. This is gold; this invention actually repels mosquitoes.

If the bad fairy appeared at the foot of my bed with the saw-brier switch, and told me the choice was to either go back to citronella or to muzzle-loading flintlocks, my only question would be to ask if my ramrod could have a silver band with my initials on it.

Next in importance, after you get past the repellent, is the seat.

Back when you put nothing under your ass but a pile of leaves when it was dry, and the *Ladies' Home Journal* when it was wet, you were not looking for comfort, but a lack of water.

No matter how careful you are, after you sit down there is going to be a root you missed, or the corner of a rock too big to dig up, that will grind into one or the other cheek of your butt at the most inappropriate times. It won't call itself to your attention when you sit down. It will invariably make itself known after the turkey gets there, or it will begin to become unbearable as time passes. Finally, in desperation, you will interrupt the business at hand to get rid of it, and will run something off you didn't know was there to begin with.

In no particular order, we have had padded flaps that had a waterproof side that hung down from the tail of the jacket, like the drop seats in old-fashioned long underwear. We have had pieces of foam rubber sewn into a length of pants leg, making a cushion 2 inches thick and 14 inches long. Adequate, until you had to move quickly and more than once, and at the end of the scramble forgot which of the two or three trees you used you left it under. This expedient worked, but was not waterproof. I remember a rubber seat that you blew up that was better. But you had to fold it to carry it and sometimes, after the fat businessman's quarter-mile dash, with shotgun, to get to a gobbling turkey, it took all the breath you could summon up just to use your mouth yelper. There was none at all available in reserve to blow up cushions.

The year before last, in Clarke County, one of the guides had a seat that one of his clients had given him that defends your ass against all enemies, foreign and domestic.

It is an aluminum tubing frame about 18 inches square. The front legs are about 4 inches high and the rear legs 2, giving the seat the high-in-front, low-in-back configuration you have in the normal chair. The seat is of woven nylon straps like the seat of a lawn chair and the thing comes with a leather carrying strap. It weighs around 2 pounds, and costs $39.95, as I recall it.

Stay pinned down for forty-five minutes by one of those gobblers that is in display, knows you are there, and is trying to get you to come that last 50 yards by strutting and drumming in one spot, and you could move the decimal point one place to the right and it would still be a bargain.

You have to remember to pick it up and carry it as you go, but if you tie the carrying case for your net underneath the legs, it will go on your back and you can carry the net and the seat as one unit.

Afternoons, when you are going to stay in one place for an hour and a half or more, and get under a tree wide enough to support your whole back, you can get a night's sleep on the thing. Or at least that part of last night's sleep you missed, sitting up over the whiskey.

We have come so far from the aspirin box, the five shells, and the *Ladies' Home Journal,* and there is so much good stuff for sale that you simply have to try out, that we are approaching the point of needing a batman, like colonels in the British army.

Lay out on a single table all the things you carry in your pockets, pouches, and vests, and those of us who are not in the financial position to employ a gentleman's gentleman really ought to have a checklist; like the takeoff checklist in the cockpit of multiengined aircraft.

Robert Rogers, who commanded a unit of Indian fighters called Rogers' Rangers, on the old Northwest Frontier before the American Revolution, had ten rules for military units. Rule One was pointed, straightforward, and elegant in its simplicity: "Don't never forget nothing."

Looks to me as if we have come to the point where if we are going to follow Captain Rogers's guidelines, we are going to need a little help.

9

INDIAN GUIDES

By the middle of April, the part of the season that belonged to me alone was gone. The balance of the time, with only a quick interval here and there, was going to be devoted to my avocation, that of Indian guide.

Indian guiding is usually fun, although there have been some moments. At this stage of my career, it is more pleasant to introduce people to turkeys than it is to hunt alone.

To tell the truth, few of us really like it alone, and I probably hunt alone more than anybody I know. But that means simply not hunting in the immediate presence of another person. If you are not able to share your wealth with friends, if you so choose, then a lot of the juice has been squeezed from the fruit before you get it.

Suppose you had 5,000 acres of mature mixed hardwood, heavy to oak, with a good road net, ample green patches, and scattered areas of open lands for nesting, all under your absolute control.

You had exclusive hunting rights. The owner maintained the roads, planted the green patches, and paid the taxes. You even had the privilege of scheduling cutting operations to coincide with times that did not interfere with hunting, and the land-management and regeneration plans were carried out under your personal direction and in compliance with your prescription.

It cost you nothing. The owner simply gave you the hunting rights in exchange for your timber-management expertise, personal charm, and scintillating conversation.

There was only one stipulation.

Nobody could hunt it but you.

No wives and daughters, no sons, no old friends, no business partners, nobody; neither chick nor child.

There are probably people who would love it, because in this world, there is some of everything. But I would rather not meet such people, even though I know they exist.

I think if I were the recipient of such an offer, I might not ever go. A time or two in the beginning, maybe, just to see what it was like, but not after that.

The example is overdrawn a little, just to make it pointed, but there is a place or two now that I can visit; and though the owner has not said so, it is clear that he thinks the invitation applies to me personally.

That, of course, is his privilege; he owns the land and is under no obligation to let anyone go there at all. But I would hunt there more frequently if, from time to time, I could share his hills and hollows with somebody else.

There used to be a thing on television on Saturday afternoon, called, as I remember it, *The Southern Sportsman.* Its theme was hunting and fishing, it was well done and featured some great photography, but it had one horrible defect.

The narrator and the guest hunters talked all the time.

Nobody ever shut up for as long as ten seconds consecutively. By the end of the first fifteen minutes, you wanted to scream, "For Christ's sake, shut up and watch the dogs."

Either of these extremes is at the ragged edge of acceptability. There is a vast area, back up there in the middle, that can be enjoyable.

To take along someone who is interested, who wants to find out what to do, and who approaches the matter with a temperament that does not require success on every trip, is fun, not duty. Properly approached, it can take you back to your own beginnings. It is necessary to approach the thing carefully, however, to keep it from turning into showing off.

From the time that all of us were little boys — and men are nothing but little boys who got bigger — we seem to have had a burning desire to show off. Some of us did it when we were very small, in which case it took the form of walking along the tops of fences in front of little girls. Even though we professed to despise them, some of the chemistry we did not yet know existed pushed us to show off in front of them.

When we got a little older, we graduated to no-hands operations on bicycles and, at an even more advanced stage, to high-speed operations in old cars, a species of showing off that sometimes had terminal results.

As is the case in so many other things he did, Mark Twain handled it better than anybody. After his dissertation on the Sunday school in *Tom Sawyer* and his description of the thunderstorm in *Huckleberry Finn*, anybody who presumes to write about either showing off or thunderstorms can save his ink.

It has already been done.

But there are some subtle forms of showing off, near relatives, genetically close subspecies, that Twain didn't get around to, and one of them is Indian guiding.

Indian guiding is, of course, a generic term. In one of its looser definitions, it describes anything done as an example, actions intended to instruct, things designed to pass on a process to another person.

A person who has his picture in the local paper with a string of fish that stretches from here to the corner of the room, or goes down to Central America and brings back a picture of himself standing behind a pile of doves half as tall as the bird boy, is not doing these things to instruct. He is doing them to rub it in.

The insinuation is that if you were as skillful as he, you would be able to call his picture and raise his bet with a picture of a bigger pile.

A white hunter in Africa is not doing the same thing at all. He is furnishing the expertise — and, in some cases, the eye — that one animal is a collectible trophy and one is not; but this is simply restricted instruction.

He is Indian guiding in the best sense of the word, but he is not trying to transfer skills. Unless you are financially able to buy large chunks of Africa, and politically astute enough to persuade emerging nations to give you a free hand with their game, you can't go home and use your newly acquired skills.

I am not at all sure that an afternoon on pen-raised quail constitutes the transmission of skills, either. It surely does not qualify a man to handle native birds, or hunt chukars in Idaho. Nor does placing a half-dozen customers in shooting houses over green patches at 2:30, and picking them up after dark and helping them drag the deer back to the truck, train a man for much of anything.

Patience, maybe. The ability to hit something the size of a calf, 100 yards away in a green patch, with a minute of angle rifle and a 6-power scope, maybe.

Showing someone how to use a fly rod, or set out decoys

and call ducks, or the mechanics of scattering a drove of turkeys in the fall, is the transmission of a process. Such activities constitute showing how, rather than showing off, and in their own subtle way are far more enjoyable.

My own particular field of showing how is turkeys, and some of the characteristics of the activity seriously restrict the number of participants of the very tender ages. That is a real pity, because the youngest are the most fun of all.

Almost by definition, turkey hunting is just like 1-0 ball games. It is not so much what is happening as what could be happening, and is conducted very largely under a Damoclean sword.

Children don't want low scores. They like ball games to be 10-8, with fifteen hits a side. They want third base to look like the last turn of the quarter-mile dash, and they want a cloud of dust hanging over sliding plays at the plate at least twice an inning.

When they go hunting, they want noise and gunsmoke and action. If they don't get it, they begin to talk about "Let's throw our hats up in the air and see if we can hit them."

The Colonel's daughter was a prime example. So long as dove shoots sounded like the Normandy invasion, so long as she hardly had time to stop and drink lemonade and eat cookies in addition to her duties as pickup man, she was satisfied and would stay as long as anybody. If you took her bream-fishing in the spring, and she could use up fifty crickets in an hour and you were the one who paddled the boat, and took the fish off and baited the hook, she would stay all day. Her real specialty — her native hearth, as it were — was to be an attendee at one of those old-fashioned vine-shaking squirrel hunts. The kind that have two vine shakers, two riflemen, and a stopper man with a shotgun who stops running squirrels right at the entrance to the hole. The party uses the whole afternoon to cover a half-section of river-bottom swamp.

She wanted no specific duties at these functions, except that of overall supervision.

Children are constitutionally equipped to be regimental commanders, at a regimental parade with the band playing and a big crowd in attendance. They get bored when the regiment has guard duty.

They consider creeping around the woods in tight-lipped silence, speaking only in the kind of clipped undertones you see pro golfers using to their caddies, to be about as much fun as arithmetic.

You can make them stay with threats, which then turns a hunt into a prison sentence and defeats the purpose. In dealing with the young, you seek acolytes, not inmates.

Unfortunately, some of the grown people you Indian guide have much the same temperament as the inhabitants of the second grade, especially if they are financially comfortable and hold positions of importance in society. In our success-oriented society, it is important that the big butter-and-egg man from Cleveland have a good shoot, kill a trophy deer, and shoot half a case of shells.

All these things can be arranged. These arrangements are precisely what make those organizations that specialize in pen-raised quail, game-farm turkeys, and corn-fed ducks a success.

Personally, I don't find any of this to be offensive. Edward VII covered it beautifully when he said that people could do whatever they wished, so long as they did not do it in the street and frighten the horses. I would add only that they not do it to me, but fundamentally, I cannot fault his rationale.

Wild game is not nearly as reasonable as game-farm targets; principally because they, like me, are not willing to let you do it to them. To a degree so far beyond the bounds of normal probabilities that it almost approaches the occult, turkeys lead the pack in unreasonable behavior.

Turkeys have such a genius for embarrassing high rank that it is almost impossible not to believe they do it on purpose. The turkey has not been hatched that would not run a mile to embarrass a lieutenant general, whereas the same turkey will frequently be relatively pleasant to a plain lieutenant.

Indian guiding for high rank, be it military, financial, or governmental, is always fraught with uncertainty until you have an opportunity to ascertain the thought processes of the guidee.

If he is inexperienced with turkeys, one of his difficulties is that he probably hears the same things you do, but he cannot identify the source. Since about 90 percent of turkey hunting is done with the ear, rather than the eye, the person who cannot decipher the sounds feels left out.

You will hear things that cause you to take various actions, some of them very quickly; and since he did not catch their significance, he must be dragged along without benefit of explanation. Let this happen two or three times, which is not unusual, and you begin to get looks that insinuate you may be salting the mine.

The guidee is having a conversation with himself that says, in effect, "This clown [you] doesn't hear any of this. He is making it up simply to make an ordinary, dull nature walk sound interesting."

I have had instances, later in the day, when the guidee, at lunch, or in the car going home, will turn to me and say, in his very best Clarence-Darrow-in-cross-examination tones, "Do you really hear all this shit? All this clucking and scratching and yelping you keep talking about?"

You have hell's own time convincing him that not only do

you hear it, he hears it as well. His difficulty comes from the fact that he cannot classify what he hears.

If you could anticipate a sound and call it to the guidee's attention before the fact, it would be a tremendous help. Since you cannot do this, you must stay as close as possible so that you can discuss sounds you have already heard, in an attempt to get him prepared for a possible repetition.

While the two of you are walking along a woods road or going to a turkey you have heard, it is impossible to get close enough to explain. After the two of you have sat down and are hidden, it becomes not only possible but desirable.

I have formed the habit of sitting at the guidee's left, if he or she is right-handed, putting my gun on the ground behind the tree, and being in position to whisper in his ear throughout the engagement.

Marvelous as it is, a turkey's hearing has dead spaces in its range of pitch and timbre. A plain whisper, spoken without hissing like a leaky boiler, is perfectly possible. You can keep up a running series of instructions as to what is happening, even to the point of telling him when to get the gun up, and even have him pull the trigger on command. You can literally talk the turkey right up to the gun.

Sitting this close has another advantage as well. Unless he pulls out his pocket pistol and does it with that, the guidee cannot shoot you by mistake. You cannot shoot yourself in the left ear with a shotgun of conventional length, and your eyes are within 6 inches of his left ear.

I do not make a practice of this business of sitting 30 yards behind the man with the gun. No communication is possible from there, unless you both read minds, and inside 85 yards, in the heavy-breathing zone, you have the period of maximum excitement. Unless you are close enough to encourage your guidee and keep him calm, he can begin to twitch and fidget and spoil everything. Or, worse, wheel around on a wounded turkey or turn to hurry his second shot, and present you with 2 ounces of fours at 30 yards, rather more quickly than you would want and at a velocity substantially above the comfort level.

The only disadvantage to sitting on his shoulder is that if he is a she, you have to point out gently that you are sitting this close to facilitate communications; there is no intention on your part to snuggle.

Indian guiding is a type of showing off, of course, but it has some saving graces. You are inflicting the breadth of your experience upon another person, but in the overwhelming majority of cases that person has asked for the infliction, and in some cases has paid for it.

There are some unpleasant people, generally the type who brags about killing fifty doves in an afternoon at cocktail parties, who take up turkey hunting. You meet some of them, but almost always early in their turkey-hunting careers. Very few of them last long enough to have lengthy turkey-hunting careers. The crowd who think the hunt a failure if they do not kill a limit in the morning, and then go back out and shoot another in the afternoon, fades away pretty quickly.

Unless you are C. L. Jordan, with over 2,000 turkeys to your credit, you are going to have dry spells, and some of them are going to be lengthy. People obsessed with numbers cannot stand this. They consider their manhoods affronted by unsuccessful hunts, and they either take up car-window and boat-seat hunting, or begin to specialize in game-farm turkeys or Texas turkeys, shot with rifles from droves of 200 on their way to water holes.

I am delighted to have them out of the boat. They breathe up air and drink water for which we have better uses.

Until the first time I went to Westervelt, I never knew how many of the right kind of people there were.

More than fifteen years ago, an old classmate of mine who

worked for Gulf States Paper Company called me and asked if I could pull them out of a hole. Gulf States runs a paid hunting lodge in Pickens County, Alabama, and had, for some years, begun the season with a turkey-hunting school. A series of events had put them out of instructors, and he wanted to know if I would come up and help with the school.

If old school tie had not been old school tie, I would have come up with some kind of excuse. It was my opinion at the time that these were game-farm turkeys. Not that there is anything illegal or immoral about game-farm turkeys, but both me and Edward VII think they scare the horses.

I have had a little experience with game-farm turkeys. In many cases, such turkeys are released at A and fed at C. The hunter and his guide are positioned at B, and the guide begins yelping at the time the turkeys are released. The yelping does not do a bit of harm. In point of fact, the guide could stand up and wave a bedsheet, and it would do no harm at all. The turkeys are going to C. Period, end of incident.

Places like this abound with stories of turkeys being found on the ground at daylight, with wives of visiting vice presidents killing 25-pound gobblers on their first hunting trip, with turkeys being killed that still have a string tied to one leg. Like I say, a scared horse everywhere you look.

But when you owe, you owe. So I went, with my tongue so far in my cheek that it sprained tongue muscles. I have never been more pleasantly surprised in my life.

These are honest-to-God wild turkeys that have been yelped to by some of the fanciest talent in the state. The only thing a customer is promised for his money is fresh air and sunshine; and if it rains, he doesn't even get the sunshine.

I would not have believed there were enough people who were willing to pay so much money for such thin chances of success, but there are, the school is thriving, and so is the regular season around the school. It tends to renew some of your faith in human nature and pick up and dust off an illusion or two you thought may have been damaged beyond repair.

Except for the very few scorekeepers, the clientele are a delight to be with. They have read enough about turkey hunting, or have talked about it to the extent that they come to the school recognizing that it is going to be difficult. At the first session, I usually make the remark that we should all understand one thing: No one present can possibly be either very busy or very important, or he would not be able to waste three days doing what we are all doing. Invariably, from among the few who do not laugh, come the score-keepers. Almost as invariably, the ones who have the most fun and get the most out of the school are the big-game hunters: people looking for trophies or quality experiences, rather than numbers. They think right, and thinking right makes them a pleasure to be around. There are few enjoyments in life as pronounced as that of being present when a man kills his first turkey, and shaking his hand, and spending the next hour listening to him tell you again and again how he did it.

At the school and during the rest of the season, during the regular hunts, a client is furnished with a guide for all the morning hunts, unless he asks specifically not to be. During the afternoon hunts, he is left on his own.

Very few of the people who hunt there realize it, but the finest addition they could make to their education would be to watch what the guide does, and ask him afterward why he did it.

I do not include myself in this august company, and not through any fit of false modesty either, but with a cool recognition of the facts. These guides, and some few others who operate in the Southeast, are the best in the world.

The staff at Westervelt, the staff whom people use at private camps like Scotch Lumber Company's, the local regulars whom Westervelt uses during the season, the group whom

T. R. Miller Mill Company used to use at Dozier Camp, and some people whose names I don't know but whom I know exist, operate in a different league than most of the rest of us.

These guides come in all sizes, shapes, and colors, although few of them are under thirty-five because they have to have been at it long enough to get competent. In certain instances, they have had an extensive background as poachers. Over the years, the establishment has found that the only sure way to get them on the side of the angels was to put them on the payroll.

They are invariably local, in many instances have farms or cows or businesses outside, and guide only as an avocation. What makes them so noteworthy are the difficulties they must operate under.

In the first place, they take out a different person nearly every day. Some of the people they take are experienced hunters; but, in most cases, they get the inexperienced end of the stick, because after they get a modicum of experience, the good guys want to try it on their own.

It is not twice as hard to hide two people as it is to hide one, the difficulty is at least squared and may be cubed. Most of the time the person they are guiding has to be told almost everything. Frequently he is not in the peak of physical condition, and often he has sat up the night before over the cards and the bottle and is a little hung over. Some of them cough; some of them smoke; most of them wiggle. All of them, in one way or another, are customers, and you cannot follow the dictum that the customer is always right if you offer to slap the shit out of him if he won't sit still.

And principally, except for a brief time at the beginning of the season, these guides never get an undisturbed turkey to work.

Somebody — usually several somebodies — has been to

him and yelped to him and run him off two or three times. Sometimes he has been shot at.

None of this has given him the relaxed, restful attitude you get from a month in the country; and you can bet your last dime he is not going to come running up, gobbling every time you yelp, like the turkeys do on those VCRs that equipment manufacturers sell in local sporting-goods stores.

It is nearly a marvel that these guys ever have a successful client. The fact that their success ratio is as good as it is only strengthens your belief in miracles.

Turn them loose on undisturbed turkeys, with nobody to hide but themselves, and nobody along who has to have his hand held, and you would have to handicap them with Panama hats, white linen suits, one hand tied behind their backs, and a two-week season to keep turkeys off the endangered list.

On April 13 I traveled to Westervelt to begin the first of this year's two schools. In the scouting that afternoon, there was sign everywhere I went, but no sightings, no gobbling, and nothing was roosted.

I am never concerned with a lack of sightings; in fact, I feel better without them. There is infinitely more comfort in finding dusting areas, gobbler droppings, gobbler breast feathers, and, best of all, wing marks on both sides of tracks in the road, where turkeys dragged their wing tips while strutting. All these signs mean there are gobblers, they are working in that area, and you probably have not run them off. I would far rather see such signs than run two or three old gobblers out of every green patch the road crosses.

The next morning, April 14, with a client, we heard one turkey gobble twice, way south of the edge of the field where we stood waiting for daylight. And when I say way south, I mean right out there on the ragged edge of imagination.

I don't think the client heard the first one, but I know he

heard the second because we had closed the distance the better part of a half-mile when the turkey gobbled again, so far away still that it gave you the nasty suspicion that it was not the same one, but a different turkey in the same direction but at a far greater range.

And in those two sentences, I have already described the best part of the hunt, because between then and 8:30, it consisted of walking, calling, hawking, cawing, and owling along probably 3 miles of road. The whole exercise reminded you of throwing rocks down a well half-full of feathers. You didn't even get to hear the rock splash or thump in the bottom of a dry well. Like the imaginary rock, the calls just disappeared into the void.

After breakfast I waylaid two or three of the guides who had taken other people, and they had had just as good a hunt as we did, although one of them had heard only one ephemeral gobble instead of two.

There was a turkey killed that morning that gobbled classically and came quickly, but the day ended with the score at turkeys 18, hunters 1. This happens a good deal and doesn't tempt anybody to fall on his sword. The degree of success is not directly proportional to the height of the pile of dead turkeys at the foot of the steps at breakfast.

But you do expect to hear of engagements.

People should hear turkeys and go to them. There should be conversations exchanged. There should be tales of gloom and disaster in the last part of the approach that you can listen to, comment on, and exclaim over sympathetically.

The afternoon of April 14, which, as far as I was concerned, had exactly the same degree of nail-biting excitement as did the afternoon before, one of the hunters brought in two eggs that looked as if they had been pecked open by crows. Each shell had a quarter-sized hole in the side and it was the opinion of the professional biologists present that crows had done the deed. I have not seen enough predator-eaten eggs to have a valid opinion.

According to the calculations I had made two weeks ago, we were supposed to be in the height of the second peak and nearly to headache time. That meant these eggs came from either a completed clutch, or one very near completion. In either case, hens should be very nearly at the point of incubation.

Never mind the signs and never mind the eggs. On the morning of April 15, as pretty a day as you could order up, we heard one turkey gobble, one time, on the ground at 7:00, nothing from the roost, and nothing beyond that single gobble on the ground no matter how much heart and sincerity I put into my yelping.

On the way out of the woods at 8:00, we parked the car and mounted one final forlorn hope. Nearly on the bank of the river there is a green patch called the walnut field. Walking down the road to that field, I thought I heard geese calling.

I have a doctor friend who tells me that when medical schools discuss diagnoses, they remind you to be sure to consider time and place. As he put it, "If you are in Alabama and you hear hoofbeats, think mule, not zebra." In late April, geese are supposed to be approaching Hudson's Bay, not hanging around in Pickens County, Alabama. But as we approached the clearing from the east, two Canada geese flew across the road, calling, and as they got somewhat to the south of us, were answered by a gobble from the ground.

We stepped to the side of the road and set up, and heard no more gobbling, but from time to time, as I continued to call, we were answered by geese.

South Alabama has begun to have an increasing resident population of Canada geese. Several areas have so great a population that there was an open season, by county, last fall. If you believe 10 percent of the stories that come out of Camden, Alabama, about depredations in flower beds and goose shit on lawns, there needs to be a spring honking season as well.

Since I have not yet mastered turkeys to the extent that I have become blasé, and after all these years of vanilla, vanilla, vanilla, would like to try a little strawberry, I am not yet prepared to drop turkeys and take up geese. But there are some points of similarity.

The honking appeared to be more vigorous in answer to a "lost" call than it did to a plain yelp or a contented cluck, but at this point I cannot really go on record as recommending either. Since my experience at this time is restricted to a constant, recurring series of one observation, there is hardly sufficient data to allow me to give advice with any degree of confidence.

But for the past few years I have been invited to Arkansas to hunt ducks and geese, and this year, if invited again, I intend to continue the experiment. Next year at the school, I will try to go a day or two early; and after that, having a total of two springs and one fall under my belt, might be in position to make some positive contribution.

On the way back to the lodge and while engaged in packing to go home I took the trouble to recapitulate the position. What it amounted to is that after two mornings and two afternoons in a place as full of turkeys as the lands around Westervelt Lodge, I had heard more noise in fifteen minutes, from Canada geese that should have been on the south shore of Hudson's Bay, than I had heard in forty-eight hours from a heavy population of native turkeys on their home ground.

Never mind all those careful calculations about the beginning of the incubation and the advent of the headache season. Somebody somewhere was adding up two and two and getting thirteen.

10

ETHICS

When I was recalled to active duty for the Korean campaign in 1951, I went back in with one of the old-line National Guard battalions from Alabama.

The battalion had been in existence since the Civil War, when it was the Fourth Alabama Infantry, and had been activated for every subsequent emergency thereafter.

As of this writing, Alabama has more people in the National Guard than any state in the Union. Not only on a per-capita basis, but more people numerically. It was nearly that way in 1951.

Between World War I and World War II, the Alabama National Guard operated in a manner that, as I understand it, resembled those territorial regiments of the British army. It was part military organization, part social club, and was nearly a synonym of permanence. A man joined a battalion for life. Memberships between the wars were controlled by those people who were already members of the battery. A recruit was proposed, there would be a meeting complete with discussions pro and con of the candidate's background and possible suitability, and then a secret ballot. Elections were not strictly democratic, but operated on the blackball principle.

Out of a total head count of ninety-six men and eight officers, the officers and the dozen people in the top three grades of noncommissioned officers usually constituted the selection team. Upon occasion, one or two of the second lieutenants would be so new that his opinion was neither sought nor considered; callow youth was not welcome in the selection process. The blackball was used to hide the identity of any of the junior members who happened to vote differently from the battery commander.

Like banks of that era, batteries in rural Alabama made decisions largely on the basis of family. Not on the basis of family wealth particularly, but on the basis of the Anglo-Saxon work ethic.

Did a recruit's family own its own farm? Did it care properly for its animals? (Artillery batteries were largely horse drawn until 1938 or so.) Did the family pay its bills? Had any member served time in prison? Time served for minor incidentals like making whiskey or killing another man in a fight did not count; the transgression had to be serious.

Matters in these respects qualified the boy on the basis of background; it was accepted nearly universally that his thought processes would follow those of other members of his family.

The qualifications of the boy himself were almost wholly physical. In most instances, he was going to come into the battery as a cannoneer or a horse holder. As such, he was going to be required to sweat a lot and do all of the heavy — and most of the moderate — lifting. If he came with the agility to play on the battery baseball team, so much the better. But the principal scope of his duties would lie in shifting trails, humping ammunition, and digging holes of one kind or another.

After family, the battery was looking for two qualities: biddability and bulk. Like St. Ignatius Loyola, the founder of the Jesuits, and his comment that he needed the boy only until he was six to train him for life, it was the battery's belief that given family and the two Bs, they could create soldiers.

Promotions were glacially slow. Battery C, at Evergreen, for instance, had records of an officer who remained a second lieutenant for fourteen years.

Batteries held dances, had ball teams, ladies' auxiliaries, and, in many cases, private bank accounts, the result of legacies left by former members. When Battery A, at Greenville, built a new armory after the Korean War, they built it on land the battery had inherited from a deceased member.

In 1951, all the officers, a healthy majority of the noncoms, and a good sprinkling of the men had been on active service during World War II. The first sergeant and the supply sergeant were veterans of World War I as well, and, before that, the supply sergeant had gone to the Mexican border with John J. Pershing in 1916. He is the only man I ever served with who had been to the Mexican border and when he was in Mexico, his regimental commander was an old gentleman who had been an underaged rifleman for Stonewall Jackson.

Since I rose to command the battery while this man was still supply sergeant, it makes me the last commander of a man whose first commander worked for Stonewall Jackson. I might ought to be inside an iron fence on the courthouse square, labeled as a national monument; but if it is all the same to everybody, I would prefer to be allowed to die before the honor is conferred.

Since these distinguished old sergeants, people like the chief of firing battery, the battalion sergeant major, and the mess sergeant were roughly in their middle fifties at the time, and I was twenty-four, twenty years later, when I commanded the battalion, there would be a familiar scenario at nearly every command inspection.

After the inspection one or two of the young enlisted men would come up and introduce himself, and say, "Colonel, Grandfather said to be sure and say hello to you, and to say hello for him, too."

And we would have a conversation about Grandfather, and how was his health, and what he was doing with himself.

I had been having Father-says-hello conversations for some years. Grandfather-says-hello does two things.

It makes you feel old enough to have pulled KP at The Last Supper or have been road guard for the Three Wise Men, and it gives you a solid feeling of continuity. It is as if every man who had ever served in the battalion still had molecules in place, and it gave you an explanation of the reason why some of the faces looked the same as faces had looked a generation ago. It is because genes can't change very much in one generation.

This continuity, this feeling that we have all been here forever, was without question the finest disciplinary tool imaginable.

A young man with any sense of family at all is going to be severely wounded when it is pointed out that his father would never have done such and such a thing. He is going to be devastated when it is insinuated that his grandfather would have considered him a candy ass. Especially if the man making the insinuation happened to have served with his grandfather.

All of which is about as good a working definition of ethics as I can come up with.

Ethics are actions you don't take because they would

disappoint somebody. Or actions you do take because you know that particular person would approve.

And it is a matter of complete indifference whether the person who would sit in judgment is present or absent, or is even alive. Dead disapproval counts, too.

Nor do ethics have a whole hell of a lot to do with what the law has to say about things. Either way, really.

It is not folklore that rural juries all across the South, sometimes in a manner almost formal in structure, attempt to ascertain, before they consider the evidence in a murder trial, whether or not the deceased needed killing. Which is why, in Alabama, it is so much more common to go to jail for stealing hogs. Nobody ever heard of a hog that needed to be stolen.

I had a friend, now deceased, who honestly felt it was more ethical to jacklight a deer than it was to shoot one that, as he put it, "Only came into the patch to get himself a mouth full of green grass."

One of the most flagrant game-law violators of all time, he found nothing inconsistent in being bitterly opposed to the practice of baiting turkeys. In his mind, both the green patch and the scattered corn constituted breaking bread together, and the basic principles of courtesy and hospitality forbade gunfire at such times.

The fact that the state of Alabama disagreed with him was immaterial. The state finds jacklighting to be illegal and hunting over green patches perfectly legitimate, but Adrian, like Steamboat Johnson, called them like he saw them.

You get to wandering down the pathways of ethics, and you find yourself making some strange choices and getting into and out of bed with some unusual opinions.

Lately, it has become fashionable not to shoot yearling gobblers in the spring. Just as it is now unfashionable to hunt turkeys in the fall in Alabama. This last is not true all across the country.

THE   SEASON

There was an article in one of the national magazines recently, about shooting hen turkeys in the fall in New York State. Turkeys that had been scattered by dogs.

The state of New York finds this to be perfectly acceptable behavior, legalizes all three actions, and has no compunctions whatsoever in talking about it in public. There are even advertisements, again in national magazines, that offer paid hunts of several days' duration to do exactly that.

The people who offer these hunts include pictures that accompany the articles and advertisements. In these pictures of the hunters, the dogs, and the dead hens, no faces have been airbrushed out, and no names have been changed to protect the guilty.

My grandfather used to say that it was impolite to find fault with the religious rituals of heathens, and of course he was right. On such grounds, I must make no comment at all, other than to take a solid satisfaction in the fact that none of the people in these pictures are blood relatives of mine.

To a large degree, we are all colored by our background, and I am aware that there are different sins for different sinners. Hunting turkeys with dogs would be a matter of utter indifference to some people in England who would turn purple and sputter at the very thought of shooting foxes. And a great deal of this whole field of acceptable-versus-unacceptable behavior changes with the generations.

A hundred years ago, before game laws had been invented, turkeys were shot in August. Turkeys shot the 1st of August would be ten weeks old, would weigh probably 3 or 4 pounds, and would roughly equate to what used to be called fryers, in young chickens.

There is no doubt that they would be delicious. They were easy to kill and would come to a whistle done at the same tempo as a yelp. I am sure nobody thought any more of doing it than they would think of picking the pears when they got ripe in August.

It becomes a question of availability.

Forty years ago, I knew no one who turned down young gobblers in the spring. Forty years ago they were not called "jakes." As best I can gather, the word "jake" emigrated here from Arkansas, at about the same time that green trout in Alabama began to be called "black bass." There were damned few turkeys to begin with, any turkey called to the gun was an event, and if he was definitely a he, you gathered him in.

In 1890 we shot fryers, in 1950 we shot young gobblers, and in the 1990s we save the jakes until they are old enough to gobble, and prefer to shoot them in the spring.

Nobody was wrong then; nobody is right now. Clearly we have done a presentable job of preserving and increasing the resource, and so long as we do that, there are no villains, with or without dogs, even in New York State.

My personal preference is that turkeys ought to be moderately hard to gather, but not impossible. It depends upon your definition of moderation, because, like *in vino veritas,* there is in moderation, class.

There is nothing in the world biologically wrong with shooting young gobblers in the spring. Sometimes they gobble, even though there is evidence to suggest they are not sexually mature.

They are definitely easier, you are very probably sawing off one of your own limbs and reducing next spring's gobbling population, and there is not the satisfaction that originates in the bone marrow that comes from calling up and shooting mature gobblers. My personal opinion is that shooting spring jakes is far more socially acceptable than sitting over chufa patches.

Green-patch and chufa-patch sitting is perfectly legal. To

begin with, a green patch makes a deer hunter feel at home. Besides, it is a splendid substitute for the deer dog.

A green patch does not run off and stay lost till next Thursday. It must be planted and fertilized, but it does not eat, runs up no veterinary bills, and does not require a license. A dog can run across the property line and run somebody else's deer back on your side of the line, but he is a trifle noisy when he does it. A green patch can attract deer across the line with a good deal more subtlety.

A chufa patch does the same thing for turkeys that a green patch does for deer, only more so. Once a turkey has been introduced to chufas, he becomes positively irrational. He visits them regularly, scratches in them exhaustively, and will even go back and rescratch in a last-year's field that has not been replanted, as if for old time's sake.

Once a flock gets used to a chufa patch, its visits are not as regular as clockwork, but they are mighty regular. A person with unlimited patience — about the equivalent of that of a deer hunter who can sit and look at the same green patch from 1:30 till dark — can shoot a lot of turkeys. He can't shoot as many over a green patch as he can over chufas, but it will serve. This state requires only that the shooting house, if used, not be elevated.

Put it on the ground, stock it with magazines and periodicals, have a soft cushion in your rocking chair, which ought to have wide armrests; they hold the wineglass better. You have to listen to your tape player with earphones and you shouldn't listen to anything like Offenbach's Overture to *Orpheus in the Underworld;* it makes you rock too quickly and tends to spill the wine in your lap. Thus suitably equipped and located, you can shoot as many turkeys as anybody.

You can win length-of-beard contests, have pictures of yourself standing over 18-pound gobblers in the local papers, and make a real cliffhanger out of the tale you tell in the barbershop, about calling him across a swamp 2 miles wide.

Of course you did. Here is his picture.

There is rather a lot of this going on. I get letters all the time from people who tell me that they have taken up turkey hunting recently, what a delight it is, enclose a picture of them on the front porch of the clubhouse, sometimes with a friend or two, and everybody in the picture is smiling except the turkey. A fair sprinkling of the letters close with the comment that next year they are going to start trying to call them, and would I care to recommend a good call and an instructional tape.

Again, there is not a single illegality anywhere in there. There is not even a bent ethic.

What you are doing here while maybe not specifically being tended to, is substituting waiting for working.

Go to any one of these released-quail operations, and you will be tended to. You don't see it being done, but somebody went out before you got there and put out the quail. Somebody else got the wagon ready, the modified cotton wagon with leaf springs and pneumatic tires, pulled by a picturesque gray mule and driven by a charmingly white-haired old family retainer with an Uncle Remus accent.

Somebody trained the dogs before the fact, and somebody will clean the birds after it. In point of fact, the ones you take home were already cleaned and frozen before you got there.

The other guys in the wagon — other than Uncle Remus, that is — are not going to talk about how nobody got to shoot doubles because the coveys couldn't stay aloft long enough for you to get in the second shot.

You make two contributions to the affair. You write the check and you pull the trigger.

A perfectly legitimate business, lots of good fresh air and

sunshine, friendly companions, a relaxed bourbon-and-water back at the lodge after the hunt, and a gourmet dinner.

Everybody has a splendid time but the mule, and he is making a hell of a lot easier living than he would pulling a plow.

There are two differences between this kind of hunt and sitting over chufa patches waiting for turkeys. One of them is the mule and wagon, and the other is the cast of characters.

You usually sit over chufas alone, and if you do, the reliance for an accurate accounting of what actually occurred must rest upon your unsupported word.

With no evidence at all, neither corroborating nor conflicting, some of the stories that come from green fields and chufa patches approach the spectacular. Most of the chufa-patch stories neglect to mention the presence of the chufa patch in the breathtaking account of the skill and expertise that preceded the culmination.

Car-window turkeys, boat-seat turkeys, turkeys running in front of dogs in deer drives, turkeys baited until the day before the season, and then shot the day after the bait was removed, all have one common characteristic. You can't look at the dear departed and tell what he was doing when he was shot.

This is what Shakespeare was talking about in the "Seven Ages of Man" speech in *As You Like It,* when he wrote the line about the soldier "Seeking the bubble reputation / Even in the cannon's mouth." It is apropos right here.

Most of the really good ones — most of the old-timers — talk more about the ones that got away than they do about the ones in the back of the truck. The comment "he whipped my ass again" is generally made with tones of rueful admiration, but admiration nonetheless sincere despite the rue.

In between the beginner and his fixation with numbers, and the old hand with his relaxed acceptance of the situation, there is a dangerous age. It happens generally somewhere in the vicinity of the two-dozenth turkey and, when it happens, there is no cure but to let it run its course.

Otherwise, perfectly ethical people become convinced that they are supposed to kill turkeys. Let two or three weeks of the season go by without scoring, and the first creeping fingers of desperation are felt. Let this go on for another week, let most everybody they know admit to success, and the creeping fingers become the clutching hand of dread.

Their manhood is at stake. They feel that word is being whispered around the clubs and lounges that Tom has lost it. What little bit he had is gone. A pity, really, but then it comes to all of us eventually.

And at this point, in an attempt to restore himself to social acceptability, one or the other of the legal but character-cheapening shortcuts is taken.

The author Ernest Gann says that there is in every man, a lesser man, and his presence smells in the sun. He is there in all of us.

Turkey hunting is not a game that needs a score or a scorekeeper and does not require the production of a dead turkey to qualify as a success. Done properly, and unscored, it is about as close to even as anything can be when one of the participants has a loaded shotgun and the other has not. To make it flat even, you would have to have as much at risk as the turkey, and you clearly do not.

But if the bubble reputation is a matter of so much importance, if your psyche keeps you awake at nights because it considers the lack of a dead turkey by the third week of the season to be an emasculating experience, there is a solution. A far more honorable and far simpler solution, that costs the inventory exactly one turkey less than does any one of the more unfortunate expedients.

Lie.

Make up some simple, unvarnished story of a two-year-old 14-pound gobbler that you almost walked up under. That you didn't have to go any distance to get to, but were already there when he gobbled. That you sat down, yelped once, and he pitched from the roost and landed in range. Mostly luck — any twelve-year-old on his second hunt could have done it.

You come out even on lies, one-to-one, you don't have to murder a turkey in a chufa patch to tell it, and nobody is going to go look in your freezer to see whether a turkey is really in there.

Think back to your days in high school, when from the conversations during study hall and at recess, it was obvious that everybody in the world knew more about sex than you did, had vastly more experience, and you had been totally left out.

They advertised back then, inside the back cover of magazines such as one called *Spicy Detective,* books with titles like *Sexual Habits of the Polynesians.* You had the sincere conviction that such volumes would correct your massive ignorance and let you join in these study-hall reminiscences without having to suffer the embarrassment of making a public confession of your ignorance.

You wanted to do this very badly, but you didn't want anybody to know about it. The magazine knew this, and knowing its clients, handled the matter smoothly. The final line of the advertisement always said:

"The postman will deliver it to the house in a plain brown wrapper, and no one will call on you."

Plain, unvarnished tales of 14-pound, two-year-old gobblers come in just such wrappers.

And nobody calls on you later.

11

FINAL THIRD

On April 17, we came to the final two weeks of the season. There was still the set of guests coming that I wanted to have a good hunt more than anybody, there was another special school at Westervelt on the last weekend, and every turkey in Alabama was imitating both the vocabulary and the speech habits of an Egyptian mummy.

The mother lode I had discovered April 1 and 2 had been reduced by three, all by other people, but an additional half-dozen replacements had been located. I knew the specific locations of twenty-six separate turkeys on 5,000 acres of land, none of which was under water. All these turkeys were alive and well, and every one of them had a roaring case of shut mouth.

There is a basic principle of tactics that says you should commit the reserve only to exploit strength, and never under any circumstances use it to shore up weakness. As cold-bloodedly accurate as this sounds, and it is just as cold-blooded as it sounds, it never prevents the weak from crying piteously for help. The beleaguered garrison never sends word to the relief column to go help another fort, and never mind bothering to come lift the siege on this one.

Turkey hunters who have favored guests arriving and nothing but silent turkeys to offer are the weakest of the weak. Tactical principles be damned; it becomes a matter of the moral principle and the material interest, and you remember what Ambrose Bierce had to say about that.

I pushed the moral principle off the log, threw AT&T into the breach, and called damned near everybody I knew.

It reminded you of those rainy February afternoons when you were almost out of wood and were trying to wring two or three cars of rotten hardwood out of an unfeeling world.

If there was a man I knew well enough to ask a favor, who had a gobbling turkey in southwest Alabama, I couldn't find him. Normally, in cases like this, you get a little help; especially if you don't cry wolf too often, and if, from time to time, you are able to return the favor.

Not this time.

I talked to landowners, to people in the wood business, to people who handled trusts for banks, to people who owned sawmills, even to people who were notoriously careless about geographical boundaries — a local euphemism for poachers — and from all this multitude got nothing but sympathy and offers no better than the opportunities I already had.

Two solid sources, friends who normally had a club turkey if they didn't have anything else, told me that they had not sat down to a gobbling turkey all year. One of them asked the name of the owner of the palmetto turkeys I had visited in Florida. Said he just wanted to hear one to prove to himself that he didn't have a psychological block.

In one particular instance, the callee became the caller,

and said if I was so sure I knew where twenty-six silent ones lived, would it be all right if he came down here to help look at the tracks.

One clown — and I am going to get even with him if it is the last thing I ever do — said this only proved his point. He has been saying all along that, over the years, southwest Alabama has had the most turkey hunters, and that we hunt probably better than other regions, on the basis of opportunity alone. He insists that we have been killing the most vocal turkeys for years and have thereby altered the gene pool. As proof, he points to the inherent empty-headedness of honey-colored cocker spaniels, caused by inbreeding when that color got so popular some years ago. He closed by saying he couldn't help, but that I should not be asking for help but should spend my time trying to get used to this instead of wringing my hands. It was going to be a way of life from now on.

With any luck at all, I am going to outlast this mental lightweight and, as a close friend of his family, am almost sure to be asked to be a pallbearer.

I am going to ingratiate myself onto one corner of the coffin, arrange to trip in an artistic fashion coming down the steps of the church, and knock the middle man on my side off his feet as I fall. If I can get to the right people, hopefully, at this point the honorary pallbearers will break into spontaneous applause. Sons of bitches do not become honorable in death. They simply become dead sons of bitches.

Alone, friendless, having been told that the relief column could not come to aid of the beleaguered garrison because they were too busy planning the battalion picnic, I gathered my tools and went up to the camp alone, one day early, to make things ready for the guests and to listen for the little voices.

There were no little voices the morning of April 18, and

no turkeys either; but that afternoon three jakes came into a recent clearing within 200 yards of the riverbank, stood around out there, and yelped at one another, at my calling, at a couple of early owls, and at a small flock of crows on their way to roost.

All three were clearly young gobblers. They were as long legged and awkward as waterbirds, had the black-tipped breast feathers and the distant tinge of pink around the eye, the double crook in the neck, and none of them had the first sign of a beard.

I would have shot any one of them on the courthouse steps in front of the governor — I was that sure of their sex. I have seen young gobblers with beards a quarter-inch long before, but usually in the fall.

I let these go by, and when they got completely out of sight, got up and closed the gap a little, and kept yelping. They yelped at me, at one another, and at every other thing they could think of until they went up to roost, and after dark, after they finally settled down and shut up, I drove back to the camp with a real feeling of satisfaction.

They might weigh 12 pounds, you might have to pick the breast to get a look at the beard, and they wouldn't have won a length-of-spur contest in a drove of hens; but they were turkeys, they were vocal, and not only did I know where they had gone to roost, but I knew the direction from which they had come. They were the best prospects in the last two weeks.

Nothing is ever automatic and a sure thing. I remember once, years ago, dropping a turkey overboard while unloading a boat onto a houseboat in the dark, and losing him after he had already been dead for three hours. Some days God bets on the other side. But considering things realistically, I was still smiling when the guests arrived.

The only explanation I can make for what happened the

next morning is that, sometime during the night, the turkeys flew down and walked away. Either that, or a panther came by, climbed the tree, and caught and ate all three of them, and carried the feathers off with him when he left.

Nothing yelped, nothing flew down that we could hear, and nothing walked by us to get back to the clearing. Mysterious occurrence number 17,482.

That afternoon, the two of us were on the north fence, where I had seen turkeys and heard a very little gobbling two weeks earlier.

We got there early enough to build a good blind and get perfectly comfortable. There was a green patch east of us and an ancient road that ran west along the edge of the woods, next to a pine plantation that used to be a Bahia grass patch. Two hundred yards north of us was an abrupt drop-off into a creek. To my personal knowledge, turkeys had roosted between the plantation and the creek and west of the green patch ever since 1966.

We were playing percentages — percentages from prior years, as a matter of fact — by establishing a partial ambush along a route that the ancestors of these present turkeys had used in other years.

A little better than yelping at tracks or old feathers, or at encouraging silences, but not a whole hell of a lot better.

We spent this afternoon there. If I had had a higher card to play, I would have played it. But simply wandering around, yelping, gave us more chance of running something off than sitting in one place.

At quarter after seven, no more than fifteen minutes before flying-up time, a turkey gobbler about the size of an ostrich walked along the edge of the woods in the road, going west — the same direction we were facing. He was level with my left shoulder when I first saw him, and he had his suspicious shoes on. He had heard the yelping, had gotten to a point where he should have been able to see the source of the noise, didn't, and was just about to go somewhere else to think about it.

One more step put his head behind a tree. I had time and opportunity to get my gun up. Dick had not driven all the way from Arkansas simply to be present when another man killed a turkey, so I brought him up to date in whispers, begged him not to move, and waited for the turkey to move far enough west for Dick to see him out of the corner of his eye.

The turkey didn't go that far. Whatever it was he saw — or heard — that he didn't like turned him around. He went back the way he came until he got so far behind us that I couldn't see him out of the corner of my eye.

The two of us sat motionless for the next fifteen minutes, and for fifteen after that, long after reason told you the turkey had to have flown up.

That has been four months ago, and I haven't heard anything yet.

It was perfectly still, not a leaf stirring, and you should have been able to hear him fly up anywhere inside a quarter of a mile. He was suspicious as hell, and edgy; but he walked off — he didn't run — and neither of us did anything to scare him further. I cannot make myself believe he would roost in a fifteen-year-old pine plantation when he had 80-foot loblolly just off his left shoulder. I think something bothered him bad enough to put him in that ground-eating trot they use, and he went to roost away back east and down by the creek. But I can't prove it.

In point of fact, I can't guarantee anything. The way things went last year, he could have walked out to the highway, flown up on top of the next trailer truck, and gone to Pensacola for the weekend.

We had two choices for the next morning. We could come

back to the scene of the unroosted trophy, or go back to where I think the panther ate the jakes.

That night, encouraged by the bourbon, we invented and selected a third choice. Go right out in the middle, stand at the edge of the swamp where we could hear anything that gobbled, swamp or hill, for 1,000 acres, and go, on the dead run, to anything that sounded the least bit like a turkey in any direction.

The next morning we successfully carried out two-thirds of the plan. We went right out in the middle, we got on the edge of the hill overlooking the swamp, and in the finest tradition of the armored cavalry, having planned deliberately, held ourselves in a state of creative anticipation, prepared to execute these plans violently. And held, and held, and held.

At thirty minutes after daylight, we quit holding. At 8:00 a.m. we decided that our owling and hawking and cawing had gotten to sound a little bit frantic, and that our walking was beginning to resemble a fidgety trot. At quarter to nine, we were frying bacon and drinking an early-morning beer back at the camp house.

The Arkansas delegation went home at noon with a frozen turkey in the cooler, an item they could have gotten at any supermarket back there. Hopefully, the company was pleasant, and the excuses were believable.

I have talked about this before, but I cannot think of a thing that is as hard to give away as a wild turkey — unless the one you give away is already picked and frozen, like the one in the cooler on his way back to Arkansas.

It is absolutely unacceptable to invite a man to hunt, and then to either shoot the turkey you roosted the day before he got there, or shoot the only one you got in range during the balance of the entire hunt.

The only ironbound road to success is to fall back to game-farm turkeys, or tethered turkeys, or baited turkeys.

It is not necessary that a guest shoot a turkey. Nobody can guarantee that without cheating in one way or another, but you ought to be able to put him in contact.

If he hears one and gets to him, even if someone had to point out the gobbling and lead him to the proper place, and the turkey gobbles at least once from the roost after you set him down, the guest has been put in contact.

If his experience level is sufficiently advanced for him to be on his own, and he hears a turkey and is able to get to it without water or geography keeping him away, he has been put in contact.

Any of the thousand and one errors that can be made in working a turkey, including getting too close in the beginning and shutting him up, do not count. He got in the game. Win, lose, or concede a draw, he got to play.

I have never kept a log, which is a pity, and I have no specifics to offer, but a turkey I have gone to, and set up on, and had gobble at least one time after I sat down, I consider to be a turkey I have worked.

If he shuts up after the first yelp, that constitutes a mistake in the working, not in the approach. One that stays, one that gobbles after you have sat down, is not frightened, has not been made uneasy, and is still trying to call hens.

If I had to estimate my success rate on worked turkeys, using the definition of worked just described, I don't know what it may be specifically, but I am confident it is no better than 2.5 out of 10.

Turkeys that walk up to your calling in the afternoon, turkeys that walk by on their way back to roost, don't count.

You can take them home and freeze them, you can have your picture in the paper, you can win the longest-beard contest at the hometown hardware store with them, but you didn't work them.

What makes the whole thing discouraging, especially to

people just taking cards in the game, is not having a chance to fool with that 75 percent, the three-quarters of the turkeys that people like me get our asses whipped by. This is the thing that makes silent seasons so discouraging.

Not that you didn't win, but the fact that you didn't get to play.

I don't know of a solution, no "little bit of sugar to make the medicine go down," and silent seasons may be one of the principal reasons why the number of turkeys in this state went from 12,000 in 1940 to 500,000 in 1990. If so, it is not a problem that needs a solution. This tendency of turkeys to go through fairly long periods when they won't even let you in the game at all may be a strength, rather than a weakness.

A turkey has a distinct penchant for secrecy, a penchant that approaches the obsessive, and it may be one of his principal virtues that he does. There are other examples.

A Carolina wren has the voice box of something that weighs 7 pounds, rather than an ounce. If a wren were the size of a crow, and had a voice box to match his size, he could break windows with the noise.

Wrens build at least one dummy nest, sometimes several dummies. Both hen and cock call the maximum amount of attention to themselves building the nests, laying the eggs, and alternately feeding one another while hatching. The fledglings are noisy, vocal, rambunctious, and when either parent arrives with an insect, set up a racket that is audible at 30 yards. By the time they are ready to fly, the whole family has made so much noise that anything in the neighborhood that does not know the event is transpiring has to be both deaf and blind. Everything a wren does is done in public.

Last spring, coming in the side entrance one afternoon, I saw a bird I did not recognize in the dogwood tree next to the front steps. I went inside, got our copy of Peterson, and came back out and sat under the carport and waited.

There were a pair of them, building a nest in one of the hanging ferns on the front porch. They went to and fro so much that with a good deal of page flipping, I was finally able to come up with an identification.

They were a pair of house finches, an introduced species from Mexico released near New York City in 1940. Peterson's description makes the statement that they are expanding "explosively." The range-limit line, as drawn on the range map, shows them to have gotten as far along as a line from South Carolina, to middle Georgia, west Tennessee, and Illinois, by 1980.

They were here on the Gulf Coast in the spring of 1995 and are probably transcontinental now.

If anything, they are even more secretive than turkeys.

The nest is built by both sexes, quickly, efficiently, and almost silently. If it had not been possible to go into the house and observe the arrivals and departures from a chair in the living room, I am not sure that the nest would not have seemed abandoned. If you sat under the carport for thirty minutes, you rarely saw a bird go to the nest site with a fragment of grass or weed. But go into the house and look through the window, and there was an arrival and departure every three or four minutes.

Plainly, they were aware of your presence and did not want to visit the nest site while you were looking.

During incubation, I can't remember seeing the hen at all. I know the cock fed her on the nest and, for all I know, may have relieved her there some. But the whole operation was silent.

After the four eggs hatched, the nestlings were as silent as the parents. Go to the nest, touch the edge of the fern basket, and all four heads would come up and all mouths open, without a sound. The pair fed the nestlings with the same secrecy with which they built the nest. In order to see much of it, you had to go into the house and look out the window.

The afternoon they left the nest, I went out to look in there to see if they were gone. We had not watered the fern since the nest building began, and when I rose on tiptoe to look in, they came out of the nest like a covey of quail, in one burst, and flew 30 feet across the yard to a maple tree.

No fluttering, no teetering on the edge of the nest, no long half-glide, half-flight down to the ground, no calling.

Just boom, gone.

All six of them were around the yard the next afternoon, in and out of trees. After that, nothing.

The whole thing was a model of efficiency, understatement, secrecy, and workmanlike matter-of-factness. Any predator looking for a house-finch lunch has to come to work early and stay late.

A turkey exhibits the same degree of workmanlike secrecy and a turkey hen, while nesting or incubating, is nearly wraithlike. It is singularly unusual for gobblers to be as silent as they were in 1995, but they were; and a turkey that does not open his mouth except to eat virtually vanishes.

He is big enough, and spends enough time in open fields and pastures, to give you some quarter-mile glimpses, and every once in a while you will drive up on one in a woods road. But when he shuts up, he effectively becomes invisible.

If, as I suspect, this has been one of the principal reasons for his explosive increase, let him be silent in good health.

12

AND FIVE TO GO

The morning of April 23rd, Shakespeare's birthday, put us into the final five days.

All the guests were gone, the final school was not until the last three days of the month, which was the final obligatory appearance, and I was left with five days for myself, or whatever part of the five days I was going to be able to handle. The days of going every morning and most of the afternoons are now behind me physically and, to be brutally honest about it, in the last eight or ten years, there has been more of season than there is of man. I can stand four in a row. After that, it tends to get a little too much like work, and I need a day off. As Dizzy Dean used to say, "We ain't what we used to be, but then, what the hell is?"

I spent the whole of the morning in the river swamp.

Swamp, along a major red-river system 60 miles from the coast, is not like the swamp that Hollywood depicts in the adventure epics, nor is it nearly as wet and inhospitable as is commonly thought.

The land along a river, where the river gets very near the coast, is called a black-water swamp. The water table is within 6 inches of the surface at high tide, and within 2 feet at low, if the land borders the Gulf. There is a natural levee near the water, extending in from the bank for 200 feet or so, that is sandy and has a variety of hardwood species. Beyond that, the ground is a slippery, black loam, accretes rather than erodes, sometimes as much as a half-inch a year, and the stand is composed predominantly of tupelo gum, cypress, some Carolina ash, and a little red maple. The understory is heavy, in places with almost as much palmetto as central Florida, and even in low water, the ground is not a suitable place to have the Sunday school picnic.

A red-river swamp, so called because in flood stages the color of the water is brown to red, not black, has distinct banks, often 6 to 8 feet high at low water, and a completely different species composition.

Along the natural levee here there is a mixture of cottonwood, sycamore, and ash. Behind this, and in some cases way behind the 200-yard-wide levee, there is a variety of species that rivals upland hardwoods in its diversity. There are fourteen or fifteen separate species of oak. There is elm, maple, white ash, hickory, red and black gum, mulberry, sassafras, hackberry, and on and on and on.

The ground is perfectly flat, and except for tupelo and cypress ponds, which may cover 100 acres, is clean, hard, has no low understory whatever, and the visibility in many places is a quarter of a mile. In winter, after the river rises, these lands are under 6 feet of water. Before the river floods, they are a delight to hunt in.

There is a thin middle story, filled with species like ironwood and swamp privet, but this is 10 feet high and there are no low briers and bushes, and no saw-brier vines. Walk anywhere you please wearing shorts, if it suits you.

There are some sloughs, which drain ponds back into the river. Early in the spring before they have dried out thoroughly, the water in them may be neck deep.

The ground will bake out hard as rock and, until it rains, which makes the top inch as slick as grease, you could drive Grandmother's Cadillac anywhere in there, except in the ponds and across the sloughs.

I was nearly eleven before I ever walked in a red-river swamp. For a boy who had spent most of his time in woods that looked the way second-growth longleaf looked in the 1930s, it was a strange world indeed.

Old-growth longleaf was almost all gone by 1940 and in its place, over thousands and thousands of acres, was about 2 cords per acre of pine whips, about 4 cords of hill red oak, and a mixture of blackjack, bluejack, turkey and dwarf post oak, with no merchantable volume, at about 100 stems an acre.

There were stands of pine scattered here and there, and a few large sawmills had reasonably stocked lands. But the state as a whole was miles and miles of miles and miles. Timber cruisers operated singly, there wasn't enough timber to require the use of a tallyman, and, quite often, a compass shot on a prominent tree, growing above the scrub oak, was visible across four or five plots, a distance of one-quarter of a mile.

The standard expected of cruisers was 4 miles of cruise line a day, and in the conditions that existed at the time, it was not an unreasonable goal.

Most river-swamp timber had been high-graded to death. Cutting there was done almost wholly on a diameter-limit basis, and over a period of time, diameter-limit cutting does horrible things to the gene pool.

Whatever combination of genes put increased height and diameter on a tree called it to the attention of the logging crew because they got it up into the larger diameters more quickly, and, once there, it became eligible to be cut and it was.

Do this for thirty or forty years, and you have a perfect example of genetic discrimination — in the wrong direction. Making hamburger out of a succession of herd bulls is no way to improve the bloodlines.

But to a boy raised on open scrub-oak hillsides, hunting quail, that first visit to a river swamp was a visit to another planet indeed. The fact that the timber was of poor quality, had excessive rot, bad form, and lousy size-class distribution was immaterial. I didn't know enough about such things to recognize them when I saw them.

What I saw was large trees, leaving out the fact that most of them were cull, at a volume of 4,000 feet per acre, that cast a total shade, had no understory at all, and a swamp that was stiff with acorns. Being stiff with acorns, regardless of the fact that most of them came from rotten, crooked, water oak, meant that it was also stiff with squirrels.

A lot of this early imprinting stuck, and is there today. I still go down into river swamps with a real feeling of expectation. I am convinced that nothing but good is going to happen in there.

They are at their finest just before dark. The owls have begun, there are wood ducks going to roost, squirrels are at their most active, deer are beginning to move around, and if it is fall and turkeys are flying up to roost, there is as much going on as there is at a three-ring circus. There ain't enough of you to be able to enjoy it all. You have to concentrate on some and leave some for tomorrow.

It is perfectly possible to have a good swamp road net but it is necessary to surface the roads with clay-gravel. Slough crossings can be either culverts or rock fords, with culverts being the most common, but crossings are required.

While not as high as normal, the water last January and February came up very quickly. In such cases, sometimes the approaches to a culvert will be blown out by current. You will have a perfectly good gravel-surfaced road, with a ditch completely across it 4 feet deep and 10 feet wide. In that case, I use an item not commonly found in the table of equipment of the average turkey hunter: a girl's bicycle.

I first heard of the use of a bicycle last spring, from a friend of mine. He hunts in an area that has an excellent road net, and he hunts most mornings before he goes to work. He points out that the bicycle is quiet, efficient, will allow you to move to a gobbling turkey very quickly and over a long distance, assuming you can hear him, and is a perfect device for covering a lot of ground trying to force a gobble out of something that did nothing on the roost and is down on the ground.

He stressed the use of the lady's model because he said it was easier to get on and off, with no central bar to have to swing your booted leg over when you mounted.

I listened, made a couple of smart-ass remarks like "Is it obligatory to have pink tassels on the handlebars?" and asked advice on what to say to the first man you pedaled up to on your way out of the woods. I filed the suggestion under the category of dead and extraneous information.

Two weeks later, I noticed that one of the guides at Westervelt had a bike in the back of his pickup, a bike that was modified to the extent of having a homemade gun rack on the handlebars. He told me his wife said that mounting a gun rack on a pale blue lady's bike was absolutely the cold-dead, rockhard proof that you were a redneck.

The Sunday morning of Shakespeare's birthday, I was faced with 5 miles of good road, cut in two by a 4-foot ditch at the 2-mile point, which means the road is 99.99 percent operational. The trouble with that statement is that when you strip the averages out of it, you have a 3-mile stretch of good road denied the use of any vehicle that you cannot carry across a ditch 4 feet deep and 10 feet wide.

At this point I made the transition and appeared for the first time as mounted infantry rather than straight leg.

I have appeared mounted since, in public; and while there have been the expected snickers, no one has winked at me, and none of the boys has asked me for a date.

My wife's bicycle is red, has no tassels of any color on the ends of the handlebar grips, and does not have a set of those turned-down racing handlebars that make you lean way over when you pump. I have not yet attached the gun mount to the bars, but will do so by next spring. You can make it with the gun slung over your shoulder by a strap, but sometimes it is in the way — and being able to get the gun crossways across the handlebars would make things go a lot smoother.

I wish someone had told me about bicycles years ago.

They are as quiet as advertised, you can cover an unbelievable amount of ground either going to a gobbling turkey or trying to make one gobble in a variety of locations; and, while a horse would probably be as good, a horse is not as easy to borrow, must be fed during the off season, and does not fit into the back of a pickup truck as easily.

There is a cross-country bike with larger tires that is probably designed for off-road travel. From my vast background of experience in bicycle turkey hunting — six days — I can see no real reason to leave the road. You simply want to get within 300 yards as quickly as possible, dismount, and operate on foot the rest of the way.

There is nothing new in this at all. It is the classical description of dragoons — i.e., mounted infantry. Like airborne infantry, they only go to work in a different fashion. It is immaterial to the job at hand whether they ride to work, jump to work, or walk to work. They are supposed to function as infantry after they get there.

Clever new ideas notwithstanding, I heard nothing at daylight and spent the morning of April 23rd going all the way out to Hogan's Bend and back, clear around to Pine Log Creek and back to the point of beginning, shouting my wares like one of those traveling vegetable trucks that used to drive through small-town neighborhoods selling snap beans and okra.

Partly through stubbornness, partly because I was running out of days, and partly entranced by the new transportation system, I persevered till 10:00; but then, having sold no snap beans at all, I gave up, loaded the bike back in the pickup, and started out. I parked at the edge of a plantation, got out, and started walking across the upper corner of the plantation to get to the bluff overlooking a creek.

In a stretch of sandy road about halfway to the creek, three crows began to circle me, cawing, like they do sometimes to a turkey gobbling in the edge of a field. There, along a 15-yard stretch of the road, was an absolute maze of gobbler tracks.

A turkey had been strutting up and down along this stretch regularly. There were tracks back and forth from one side of the road to the other. Everywhere you looked, there were those wavy wing marks, made when the last two primaries are dragged during the strut.

This turkey may not have been gobbling, but he had been strutting, and it looked as if he had been doing it here on the same stretch of road ever since the last rain. Some of the tracks were almost fresh enough to still have a foot in them. That — and the fact that the crows were still hanging around in nearby trees — convinced me that not only had he strutted there that morning, but it was highly probable I had run him off as I walked up.

This is like getting money from home without having to write for it. If you know where he has been most mornings, and feel confident he has not finished going there, you don't care whether or not he gobbles. In fact, you would rather he didn't. You know where you want to go, and it is unnecessary to call anybody else's attention to the matter.

I backed off into the plantation to a point within good gunshot of the strutting ground and spent thirty minutes building a first-class blind. Actually, it went beyond first-class; it was positively artistic.

I built it facing north so the rising sun would not be in my eyes, it had depth and shadow inside, and I even put up my net and put the seat inside, so that in the morning I could tiptoe silently down the road in the dark and occupy the position in utter silence without the necessity of cutting bushes. All that would be required would be to get in, sit down, shut up, and wait for company. I might tree-yelp a time or two, and I might not. It depended on what things looked like at the time and how much noise I might hear.

I got there so early on the morning of the 24th that I very nearly went to sleep inside the blind, waiting for it to get light. At daylight, three turkeys gobbled along the north fence where the plantation joined the mixed pine and hardwood, overlooking the creek.

There were three separate turkeys; one due north of me and two more, a quarter of a mile east and west of the one in the middle. They gobbled four or five times each, and any one of them was close enough to go to. This was more gobbling than I had heard for five weeks. Best of all, I didn't have to go to anything. I was already there.

Clearly, one of these was the turkey that had been parading up and down in the road in the area just in front of me. Maybe all three of them came there and strutted. There was certainly enough sign out there for all of them to have been doing it since the last of February.

All I had to do was sit still, be patient, not do anything reckless, and when he — or they — got there, simply pick out the biggest one, shoot, and pick him up.

At early flying-down time, a hen pitched out of a tree east of me and sailed overhead to land in the road 100 yards west of the strutting area and kept walking.

About two or three minutes later, two of the crows flew up and alighted in trees just above the strutting area and sat there, like they were waiting for something.

They left after ten minutes, but I waited. And waited and waited and waited. At the end of twenty minutes, I did a couple of soft, tentative yelps. As time passed and my patience grew shorter and shorter, I yelped more and more and livelier and livelier, until there at the last, with a diaphragm in my mouth and a fighting purr box in each hand, I was doing my celebrated imitation of a hyperactive Japanese turkey caught trying to pass a counterfeit bill in a Greek restaurant.

It never did become necessary to pick the biggest of the three turkeys strutting up and down the road because there never was anything out there to pick from.

At 9:00 I gave up and went home. On the way, the thought occurred to me that maybe it was just an anomaly. One swallow does not make a summer, and one nonappearance at a strutting area does not mean abandonment. The more I drove, the firmer and more complicated became my rationalization. By the time I got home, I could hardly wait for the next morning so I could get back up there and do better.

I was back the morning of the 25th, doing business at the same old stand, with the single exception that I carried in with me an armload of freshly cut bushes to stick in front of the net since the bushes stuck the night of the 23rd would have wilted.

Those of you with backgrounds in psychology can create any philosophical scenarios you choose, with analogies about wilted bushes and wilted hopes being replaced with fresh ones, so long as you do not give me the benefit of your thoughts.

I would just as soon not be exposed to them, because on the morning of the 25th, I was not exposed to the presence of any turkeys, either. They gobbled about as much as they had the previous morning. I, as faithfully, stuck to the same game plan as before. The only difference was the absence of the flying hen.

There was a hen coming down the road just before I gave up and left. She was coming toward me, would run ten or twelve steps, stop and peck at the ground a time or two at the side of the road, and then break into another run for ten or twelve steps and stop and peck a little on the other side.

She went right by, doing this, and passed out of sight east of me around a bend in the road, still doing it.

If there is an explanation, I don't want to hear it. When turkeys get into these irrational moods, it is pointless to try reason and logic. They simply are playing in a higher league. The less you concern yourself with their irrationalities, the more likely you are to retain some of your sanity.

April 25th closes the season in those counties in the state that have a fall season. About a half-dozen counties, which have had the most turkeys since 1940, still hunt in the fall, with Wilcox, a county that I thought might be the last to give up, dropping out a year or two ago.

There is no reason for this closure, except that there are more deer hunters than there are turkey hunters. Ugly, fat girls outnumber the other kind by a substantial margin as well, and these numbers (of hunters, not fat uglies) control county officials. Deer hunters feel inferior in front of turkey hunters anyhow, a kind of psychological penis envy as it were, and never overlook a chance to create trouble. These fall closures mark one of their more successful efforts.

Just exactly how a five-day reduction in the spring can equate to a forty-day season in November and December is beyond my comprehension. It must be about like taking comfort in what are called "mitigation lands."

One or another agency floods 5,000 acres of bottomland and then institutes a feverish search for 5,000 acres to be purchased with public funds in order to mitigate the loss.

Nobody has ever explained to me satisfactorily how changing the ownership of 5,000 acres from private to public adds 5,000 acres to the land base. The flooded lands remain at the bottom of the lake, lost to everybody but the fish, and the tax assessor erases the name of the citizen who formerly owned the mitigation lands and writes in the name of the government organization that is the new owner. The lost 5,000 acres remains lost, along with the taxes formerly paid to the tax collector by the old owner, and the new owners have in no instance up till now been able to get the Creator to add to the amount of firmament created in the beginning. The net result is therefore the simultaneous loss of 5,000 acres of wetlands to the land base and the financial loss to the county of the taxes on 5,000 acres. But all in a good cause, of course.

Like so many bureaucratic edicts, this gives you the same warm feeling you get when you pee down one leg.

I took the 26th off, both to rest up and to pay my respects to the lost five days denied the old-fashioned counties. On the way back up, the last day before my second tour of the year as Indian guide, I formed a different scheme of maneuver.

Damn the strutting ground and damn the indicator crows. I was going to get halfway between the strutting ground and the tree line along the north fence. I was going to go to the first turkey that gobbled, regardless of direction. I was going to go to him, get close as I could without crowding anything, and faithfully spend the morning right there.

Nothing fancy, nothing unusual. Just patience, patience, all the way, with never a sprig of yew.

The middle turkey of the three that gobbled on the morning of the 24th did it again and did it just at daylight. I had all of the time in the world to get there. The plantation is absolutely clean up to the fence, its northern edge, and I had 5 inches of pine straw to walk on and nothing to break off and make noise on the way. I got up there, found a dandy tree to set up under, looking east, with a screen of weeds at the base.

After I sat down and got ready, he gobbled once more, to ease my mind. The distance was as right as it ever gets. When it got light enough, I did one soft series of tree yelps. He didn't cut me off, gobbling before I could get through, but he did gobble right back at the call, instantly, with hardly a second between my yelp and his gobble.

Clearly he had heard me, clearly he thought I was a hen, and obviously he expected me to walk up under the tree he sat in.

By the 27th of April, any turkey hen that is going to nest, or that has not had a nest broken up, is halfway through the incubation stage. There are no groups of hens drifting around feeding, going to gobblers, spending most of the day away from the nest, except to drop by and lay another egg. Laying has been completed for two weeks, and things are quieted down. A turkey that answers a yelp at this time does not have half-acre droves of hens roaming around unattached, to come to his gobble.

It says so in the manual. Right there in the bold print.

After he has answered, I have a distinct reluctance to continue to call to a turkey that is still on the roost. As a general rule, the more you call, the more he gobbles, and the more fixed is his determination to call you to him. I have even gone so far as to do it deliberately — yelped every time he gobbled — and had him sit in the tree and gobble for an hour.

This turkey was undisturbed, he had answered, and he knew where I was. I was not going to call again, and never mind about that line about a foolish consistency being the hobgoblin of little minds.

The three of us — me, my hobgoblin, and my little mind — sat there in silence for an hour and a half. We didn't hear him fly down, he never made another sound, and we didn't see him on the ground. I could not have been an inch beyond 200 yards from him when I sat down, and except for the area immediately along the old fencerow, I could see 300 yards east in the plantation and nearly that far in the mixed pine and hardwood north of the fence.

After we gave up, I walked down the fencerow until I was about under the tree he had gobbled from and didn't flush him off the ground or out of a tree.

Your guess is as good as mine, maybe better, because maybe your hobgoblin is not as big as mine is.

In 1995 the turkeys in Baldwin County closed the season on April 25th, the same day the state closed it in the fall counties, closed it de facto if not de jure.

It had been the most silent season since 1968, and if this means it happens once every quarter of a century, I am grateful. I won't have to put up with it next time.

This season, all of it, I sat down to three gobbling turkeys, two of them at one time, the two that flew over my head in central Florida the second day, and the one this morning, April 27th.

The two in Florida, I called up. The fact that I couldn't shoot after they got there is immaterial; they were called.

I ran off the one this morning.

I called up two more that didn't gobble. The one I shot the

morning of March 21, and the one I called up the afternoon of April 19th, the one we tried to save for the next morning.

On the way home, there came to mind Mark Twain's story, in *Life on the Mississippi,* about meeting the boyhood friend who had become an actor in St. Louis. He insisted that Twain come to that night's performance of *Julius Caesar* to see him perform. Twain attended the performance, couldn't find his friend, and said so when he met him on the street the next morning.

The man was outraged. He pointed out that in the second act, there was a scene where ten Roman soldiers were on the stage and he was the second to the last soldier from the left, in the back row. That years ago he had been the last soldier, but he had been promoted.

I know exactly how he felt, except for one thing. I have been the last soldier in the back row for fifty-seven years; but if there has been a promotion, for the life of me, I cannot recall it.

13

BEHAVIOR

One of our principal characteristics as a society is our inherent belief in the principle of the transferred skill. This principle, simply stated, means that today's society in the United States believes that expertise in one field transfers itself automatically into expertise in another.

It is entirely possible that Jack Nicklaus may be the best golfer who ever lived. In matters pertaining to golf, like the purity of your swing, or the ability to concentrate, or the process of thinking out shots before you try to make them, the strategic assessments of upcoming holes — all the individual mechanics that go into making up your game — he stands alone. Nobody knows more than he, and there probably is no higher authority to whom you could take your problems.

But does Jack Nicklaus really know all that much about shirts? Of course, Jack wears shirts, and buys shirts, and does all the things other people do with shirts. But he doesn't know any more about them than you do. Golf clubs, yes, absolutely. Shirts, horse-feathers.

A set of golf clubs with Jack Nicklaus's name on them can insinuate that Jack had a hand in their design, manufacture, and sale. I am perfectly prepared to pay more money for them because I think his expertise may have some value.

Why, then, in the United States, will a shirt with Jack Nicklaus on the pocket outsell one with Joe Smith on the pocket by 126-to-1?

The principle of transferred skill.

This is why we let a movie actress with a 38-inch bust-line tell us who to vote for. It is why we let Meryl Streep be the television spokesperson during the apple fiasco when the country became convinced that alar caused everything from falling hair to fallen arches. It explains why retired pitchers can sell underwear and emeritus quarterbacks can sell automobiles. Because we believe, in our souls, that expertise in one field automatically confers expertise in all fields.

Even those of us who recognize the failing in ourselves fall into the pit, knowing it is there, knowing it is silly, knowing better all the time.

If there is a creature on this earth that specializes in secrecy, it is the wild turkey. Only in the last few years, when portable radio-telemetry became inexpensive enough and small enough to be attached to turkeys, have there been decent studies on turkey behavior that are documented properly.

Until these, we took our doctrine from gray hairs, or because the man could write a simple declarative sentence and get it published, or because he had a reputation around town as an expert and had won the biggest-turkey contest at the local hardware store three times.

The fact that every turkey he entered in the contest may have been killed over bait, or while running in front of the dogs on a deer drive, or was bushwacked from a shooting house as he walked into a chufa patch in the afternoon, never came up.

Our mentor was a turkey hunter, a contest winner, a published journalist, and he had a collection of beards and feet nailed to the wall in his den to prove it. That made him an expert on turkey behavior as well. It transferred.

Quod erat demonstrandum. When he speaks, let no dog bark.

There is a subparagraph within this principle that is even more astonishing: the subprinciple of the immortal myth.

Regardless of the weight of evidence, no matter that specific proof has been demonstrated again and again, in spite of the fact that you couldn't get the conflicting data into a 10-ton truck, immortal myths have a life of their own and cannot be killed with anything, not even with silver bullets or wooden stakes driven through their hearts.

Turkeys can't live in pine plantations. Clear-cutting destroys the habitat and absolutely destroys the breeding stock. All turkey scratching is V shaped, and the point of the V shows you which direction the drove went. If you don't plant chufas, all your turkeys will move onto the lands of adjoining owners. Yelp back every time a turkey gobbles, and he will come directly to the gun, just like those turkeys do on the videotapes. There really and truly is a call that never fails. All you have to do is get somebody to show it to you, practice it, and you will become so expert that if the Fish and Game Division ever found out about it, you would be declared against the law by name, like baited fields and live decoys.

I used to campaign against these myths until I ran out of wooden stakes and silver bullets, but I have decided it is hopeless. They truly are immortal and will outlive us all. But I do have a suggestion. Like those people who absolutely refuse to believe in evolution, but fit the evolution of species into a twisted explanation of Genesis — i.e., who can say but that what Genesis calls a day may have been as long as 30,000 years, you can take the data now available on habits and behavior, and fit it into your own collection of beliefs founded on the unkillable myths and still be comfortable.

Joe Hutto's book *Illumination in the Flatwoods* was published in October 1995. This book is absolutely unique in its approach. It comes to some conclusions on turkey behavior that have been reached as a result of a level of observation hitherto not achieved.

Joe Hutto did not simply join a drove of turkeys for six months, he *parented* a drove of turkeys for six months. Hatched them from the eggs, imprinted them as they were hatched, and then withdrew from the human race, became the brood hen, and raised the drove to adulthood.

I don't know Joe and have no notion of his financial resources, but he has to have the most understanding wife in the world, and either be independently wealthy, or have the ability to live as if he were. As you read the book, you will see that he did almost nothing else for six months but be a turkey. He did not simply raise turkeys, he became a turkey.

If you can't afford to buy the book, borrow it. If you don't have many friends and have no access to libraries, steal it. But whatever you do, read it.

There is stuff in there that explains some things I have seen happen and could not understand. There is stuff in there that I never dreamed existed. There is stuff in there that reinforces observations I had already made, and there is stuff in there that absolutely contradicts things of which I was positive.

I am not sure of them anymore. I know of no higher authority to whom I can appeal because I have only two choices.

I can choose to believe that there is no such person as Joe Hutto, that this is the pseudonym of a free-verse poet who lives in a garret on Rampart Street, who has never been in the woods in his life, and has, like Audubon's drawings of fake fish, perpetrated a scam on all the turkey hunters in the world as a massive April Fools' joke.

Or, I can believe this is an accurate and careful record of a marvelous period of observation by a man who devised a unique method of crossing the line, crossed it, and stayed there for six months, and then came back to tell us about it.

I choose B.

I am not going to either try to rewrite Joe's book for him in these remarks, or tell you that the butler did it and spoil the mystery before the final page, but there are some things that I find so astonishing I have to talk about them a little. One of these things is the ability of a turkey to recognize colors.

There has been some earlier work done on color recognition in turkeys. Some studies with a yellow, a green, and a red button, only one of which opened the spout and let the corn trickle out, and the ability of turkeys to pick the proper color no matter which end of the line it was on.

Hutto goes beyond that. He gets into preference, indifference, and discomfort, and has levels for all three. He cites a specific instance, when the poults were three days old, of the entire group huddling in one corner of the brooder when he replaced a brown towel on the floor of the pen with a bright blue one. He repeatedly observes a preference for pale blue, the blue of faded jeans, which he hypothesizes may come from its resemblance to the blue of the head of a hen, and a repeated discomfort with bright blue or purple. He states categorically that both red and purple are totally unacceptable. Turkeys regard Day-Glo surveyors' tape with caution and fear on first encounter, but if it is left in place, will finally learn to disregard it.

There are moves from time to time to require the use of blaze orange by turkey hunters, as it is now used by deer hunters. I had made up my mind before Hutto that I simply would not comply if the regulation was adopted.

Not that I would sit down and write a letter to the Director of Fish and Game and refuse blatantly, but be sneaky.

Wear it in the car, wear it in camp, if necessary wear it into the woods in the dark, and when I was finished and coming back out, put it back on. But there is no way I would sit down to a turkey wearing blaze orange. I would simply take off the vest and put it under my shirt until I got through hunting.

I have read of a study now being conducted by the state of Missouri to see what effect the use of a blaze orange band had when the hunter put it around a nearby tree before he sat down to yelp. The rationale was that a band of orange would appear to a turkey like a land line or oil-exploration tape, but it would show other hunters that the yelping came from another hunter. It would tend, as well, to make a person reluctant to slip up on an orange band in the woods, in the belief that there was a turkey yelping near a land line.

Before Hutto, I was willing to try the orange band. But now I am not going to use an orange band unless the state passes the law and then furnishes a man to go with me every day to ensure my compliance.

In my mind, Hutto's observation about faded blue putting a turkey at ease goes a long way toward explaining why so many turkeys were killed over all those years by a country-man sitting still in the woods, wearing his faded overalls.

I have been aware for years of the natural antipathy between turkeys and crows. I cannot remember the number of times crows have flown up to my yelping, circled once or twice silently, and then alighted in nearby trees and just waited, looking for the turkey clearly and obviously.

I have, just as often, seen crows diving on a gobbler strutting in an open field, gathering around him much as they do an owl. Now I know more about crows than I did before.

Hutto recounts an incident that happened early in September, when he, and the balance of the drove — to quote him, "We are fifteen now, if I include myself" — find a flock of crows feeding in the end of a small field. The turkeys become very excited and scatter in all directions, flying singly after individual crows. Both flocks — crows and turkeys — disperse, and eventually everything comes to a standoff and all flight ends. Hutto and one of the drove that did not do any chasing begin calling from the field. He says: "Turkeys, scattered over a ten-acre area, begin flying in from all around. The birds seem very proud of themselves."

When you recall how many times you flushed two or three turkeys out of trees at 2:00 in the afternoon, or single turkeys at 10:30 in the morning, and never knew what had put them up, you begin to see what ought to have been self-evident: We, and by we I mean us people, constitute a very small part of a turkey's life. We tend to think we are the most important thing of all, until you begin to think about it and look at some numbers.

A turkey is off the roost and moving around at least twelve hours a day, as much as thirteen or fourteen in the summer, which puts him on the ground and moving about nearly 4,400 hours a year. In a five-week spring season, if someone hunts every other day and stays four hours, people are in the woods for only seventy-two hours, less than 2 percent of the time a turkey is on the ground. If a hunter is in contact with turkeys for one-third of the time he is out there, he has been fortunate indeed.

Therefore, a turkey fools with people less than 1 percent of the time, hardly enough to make us a dominant factor in his thinking.

Admittedly, we are the only thing with a shotgun that he meets and consequently can be a fatal 1 percent, but there are a lot of other enemies, a lot of things that eat or bite or claw. We are only a minor portion of his troubles.

Hutto talks at length about something that can come only from repeated observations of the same turkey, or group of turkeys: their specific memory of an event and their recognition of the particular place where that event took place. It clearly works both ways; they evidently remember pleasant events as well as unpleasant ones.

He describes a pile of rotten logs the drove passes on its normal rambles, where at the age of ten weeks they discover an extremely large rattlesnake. The turkeys are frightened by the snake to the point that some of them fly and, on subsequent visits, slow down upon nearing the vicinity of the pile of logs and make a careful and hesitant approach to the pile before going by. They clearly remember the incident, associate it with that particular pile of logs, and are extremely wary in approaching the vicinity thereafter.

Certain favored loafing places are evidently recalled with pleasure. Hutto records how, upon approaching a particularly pleasant group of live oaks, near a small creek where they had spent several days nooning, some of the drove would run ahead to get there first, exhibit every indication of pleasure at being there, and have a distinct reluctance to leave.

For years, I have been aware of a turkey's ability to avoid a location where he had been frightened or harassed. But I have had considerable trouble trying to find out why a particular location is favorable. There is a location I know of that always seems to hold turkeys in the spring, and turkeys always gobble there. If one is killed, then within a day or two, another one begins to gobble in the same place. Over the years, I have nearly worn the place out trying to find what makes it attractive.

Hutto may have solved it for me. Turkeys go there for the simple reason that they like the location.

There used to be a particular ridge in lower Wilcox County that I visited regularly at lunch. It was not all that convenient. You had to park and walk a half-mile to get there, but something in the air there soothed my soul. Working in the area, I would frequently stop at a country store and buy sardines, cheese and crackers, and something cold to drink, and then move lunchtime to anywhere between quarter to eleven and one-thirty, just to arrange to go by there to eat. I just liked the feel of the ground under my feet in the place.

Evidently, turkeys are subject to the same feelings. Deliberately go out of their way to get to a certain place, take at least a moderate amount of trouble to set up a collection of time/place circumstances for the good and sufficient reason that they like to do it. They like it there.

My taste buds do not operate in a different fashion because I happen to be on the east slope of Janie Lee Mountain in Wilcox County. Sardines and cheese and crackers are just that, no matter where you eat them. But they taste better in my head, there, and I am perfectly willing to accept the fact that a turkey is capable of identical emotions.

There is a term for that. It is called employing an anthropomorphic analogy. But if we are to accept the rituals of both Baptists and Buddhists in our society, then I feel that we anthropomorphists ought to be extended the same courtesy.

But of all the behavioral characteristics that Hutto describes, of all the incomprehensible habits, of all the nearly supernatural actions, the matter of eye contact wins the gold medal.

It has been described and recorded before, for example the comment made by Lovett Williams in 1981:

> In my studies, I have approached young broods with my eyes fixed on the telemetry receiver without knowing their exact location. When the dials indicated that the radioed brood was

close by, I would begin to scan the ground in the vicinity to visually spot the brood. Despite the fact that I sometimes approached this way within thirty feet of a brood, there would be no movement by the hen or poults until I spotted them. But at that instant, escape behavior invariably ensued. I have seen this many times and have been impressed with the ability of the hen to know exactly when she had been detected and to react instantly, but not before. It was not necessary to move toward the brood to elicit escape behavior — the sense of being detected was enough.

If you don't find that close enough to a combination of voodoo and second sight, listen to Hutto:

A turkey's sensory ability clearly borders on the supernatural. . . . Two things have surprised me, however. One is how elaborate and complete inherited information is in wild turkeys, and the other is that they have well-developed cognitive abilities. It appears that wild turkeys begin with a genetic program of adaptive information and then set about gathering the details specific to their particular environment. Every day I see that the most important activity of a young wild turkey is the acquisition and assimilation of information. It is the food they are most hungry for. They are curious to a fault, they want a working understanding of every aspect of their surroundings, and their memory is impeccable. They gather specific information about a particular environment, conspicuously apply that information to a framework of general knowl-

edge, and make appropriate choices in modify-
ing their behavior. The apologies that precede
discussions about wild-turkey intelligence are
definitely not warranted. I have never observed
another animal making such a dedicated effort
to know and to understand.

There is not all that much opportunity to look birds in the
eye. Some in trapping and release or in banding operations,
and some in instances where birds have been drugged and
are in hand when the drug wears off. You get an opportunity
to look in a wild turkey's eye and you see the same thing you
see in the eyes of a first-class bird dog.

They are not simply the eyes of a dumb brute. There is
somebody home in there.

We have wandered a long way across the line here, and
nobody knows it better than me. The last thing I want to do
is to be guilty of ascribing nearly superhuman behavior to a
bird, in order to over-glamorize hunting him to the point that
when I do manage to shoot one, there should be a brass band
and a torchlight procession. I am not a Roman general, and
he is not a defeated chieftain, walking barefoot and in chains
behind the chariot.

But I do truly believe that because of a particular set of
circumstances, partly on his part and partly on mine, I have
managed to personalize him down through the years. He has
passed beyond being a bird, he has become a presence.

He doesn't just stand around out there, he thinks. But if
you let yourself believe in that too much, you run a very real
danger.

It might get too close to self-immolation. You might get to
the point where you could never shoot at one again.

14

COVEY RISE

The more of something you have in inventory, the more natural it is to be generous with what you give away.

An eighteen-year-old, with a life expectancy of sixty more years, drives his automobile as if he were not only immortal, but had the hand of God Almighty resting on the wheel to help.

Seventy-year-olds, with four or five years left on the probability tables, drive around with both hands on the wheel at ten minutes to two, hats firmly centered on their silver locks, at speeds somewhere between 40 and 45. They never had a wreck. Like Typhoid Mary, they are the carriers. They have been responsible for entire epidemics of crumpled fenders.

When I first got in the sawmill business, at the lowest possible entry level — a $200-a-month timber marker for an old-line southern lumber company — I lived in the company hotel, right behind the commissary in a company town.

A company sawmill town was like an army post. It was army/company everywhere you looked. The company did not own the post office — it was content to leave that in the hands of the United States, although it did have a lot of clout in who was appointed postmaster — but pretty much everything else in town operated, if not under its direct control, at least by its direct sufferance.

I took my meals in the hotel dining room, room and board was offered for $40 a month, transportation to and from the woods was furnished by the company. The only thing I had to handle on my own, to achieve complete self-sufficiency, was getting somebody to do my laundry.

Which is how I met Will Darden.

Mrs. Darden, whom I never met, took in washing. It was boiled in an iron pot behind the Darden house, and work khakis — both pants and shirts — came back pressed. Dress shirts, the kind you put on after work to have a beer, came back starched and ironed. The simple use of the word "starched," to describe Mrs. Darden's shirts, is insufficient. A better choice might be "armored." There is no question but that they would have turned birdshot, and maybe No. 4 buck.

I never met the lady because it was unnecessary. Mrs. Darden was manufacturing. Will was sales and marketing.

Will drove a mule and wagon and picked up and delivered once a week. Deliveries were subject to weather, because it was an open wagon, and the weekly charge was $2. I kept my room unlocked. It never occurred to me to lock it; there was nothing in there worth stealing. When something was dirty, I dropped it on the floor of the closet. Will would come in, hang the clean clothes in the closet, pick the dirty ones off the floor, and leave. I left the $2 payment with one of the cooks in the kitchen because Will always came by while I was working in the woods.

The system worked beautifully — things always do if you keep them as simple as possible — and you should not think I was taking advantage of the Darden Laundry Company. Two dollars a week was not only the posted price, it amounted to more than 4 percent of my pretax income.

Cleanliness, in addition to being next to godliness, is also right next to expensive.

Immediately after one of Will's deliveries, I became the soul of generosity.

A young man with a closet full of clean shirts, not only clean but cracklingly starched, sometimes wears two shirts a day on Monday. In addition to being perfectly willing to lend shirts, he may even ask you casually if one is enough.

By the middle of the week, he has become careful; and by Friday afternoon, he reminds you of Ebenezer Scrooge before his conversion.

Hunting days are exactly the same. First of the season you can let one go to tend to some business, if the business is truly pressing. You can stay home if it rains. You can take a day off to take the friend of a friend, or to rest up.

Get into the last week, and all the shirts are gone from your closet, the delivery wagon ain't coming, and don't ask me no questions when you see I am busy.

I went back to Westervelt for the second school, for the final three days of the season, with a closet bare of shirts; and neither Will Darden nor the U.S. cavalry was coming at the gallop to rescue the garrison.

The first afternoon at the school is spent scouting the area you have drawn. I always draw an area and look it over as carefully as I can, trying to find something for the next morning. That way, whichever student I draw from the hat, or am assigned, has the benefit of anything I may have found the afternoon before.

If in his scouting he has seen turkeys or heard them, and

his prospects seem better than mine, we go to his. If I have a hot prospect and am able to convince him that mine sounds better than his, we go to mine.

The process brings into it a degree of delicacy that bears a little bit of discussion.

When you are a beginning turkey hunter, you are exposed to instances of what appear to be casual cruelty. You will be alone in the woods for a period of time, and you will see sign, or turkeys, or both, and when you get in that night, you undertake to report what you have discovered. Older, more experienced hunters will listen to your report, sometimes exchange glances and sometimes not, and may then begin to formulate plans that completely disregard what you have just reported.

It makes you want to stamp your foot, throw a temper tantrum, and shriek, "Goddammit, I just told you where the turkeys are! Why are you talking about going someplace else?"

They heard you, they assessed the probable value of your intelligence and found it to be worthless, and they have begun to lay plans as if neither you nor your information ever existed.

Other than being discussed in the third person, when you are present at the conversation, I know of nothing that gives such a strong sense of inadequacy.

It is infuriating to have these wrinkled old clods make such a judgment when they were not within two miles of the incident reported, and even worse, make it two hours after the fact.

What has happened in many cases is that they decide what you have reported is tactically impossible. You are mistaken in your distance, where you say you were is a half-mile over the line on another owner, it was too early or too late for such an incident to happen, and basically, you don't have sufficient experience and background to let anybody waste a morning on what is almost sure to be faulty intelligence, reported inadequately.

Normally, situations like this happen to you when you are in your early teens. The general staff that ruthlessly ignores your contribution is composed mostly of blood relatives, and being as young as you are, nobody gives a rat's ass about your feelings, anyway.

It becomes just another one of the incidents that make dealing with your elders so stressful.

None of these criteria fit the students at the school. Most of them may be inexperienced, but almost all of them are successful. The price structure more or less culls out the financially disadvantaged. A lot of them come from positions of power and authority, they are used to having their comments listened to and valued afterward, and it is absolutely inappropriate to insinuate that after you have listened to their half-assed comments, you will file them.

You are forced to listen carefully, try to assess the probable accuracy of the report as rendered, and then act on whatever value it appears to have.

If the man saw a turkey fly up out of a green field, and then gobble twice from the roost after he got up there, you have a certainty. You have only to ascertain that the green patch pointed out on the map and the green patch he occupied at dusk are one and the same.

As you get farther and farther afield from certainty, and deeper and deeper into the jungle of obscurity, you may have to hedge the bet some. If the jungle is truly obscure, you may find it necessary to lie.

You lie by embroidering the report on the area you scouted and convincing the hunter that the chances of success are better there. In seasons of normality, where you can confidently expect to hear a turkey or two gobble at any place, on any given morning, there is little risk in these evasions. Even if the turkey the two of you go to is not precisely where you led him to believe it was the night before, it is a turkey, you can go to it, and success, like truth, is a perfect defense.

If the man has not heard anything, there is no problem at all. He has probably jumped to the erroneous conclusion that he drew a bad card, and there were no turkeys there to begin with. He did draw a bad afternoon, but on that place, there is no such thing as an area without turkeys.

Where you need to exercise the maximum degree of salesmanship is in those instances where you convince him you have a better prospect than he thinks he does, you persuade him to go with you, and then you expose him to a silent sunrise.

The whole exercise has an unfortunate number of thorns among the roses for two reasons. If the man were a guest of your club, then presumably you would have some idea of his level of experience and could better judge how much faith you could afford to have in his reported locations.

These people are not friends of members. They are paying customers, you met them only yesterday, and you must judge their level of expertise/reliability upon the sketchiest of data. If they have drawn your services by lot, and as a guide you were not there the day before, neither of you has a choice. You go to the assigned area and do the best you can.

The danger lies in telling a man who thinks he has heard something that, in effect, he does not know enough to assess what he saw or heard, and since you know so much more than he does, he should abandon his prospects and go with you.

The only good thing about the afternoon of April 28 was that neither I nor the man I was to guide in the morning had heard a single sound. I was not faced with the prospect of talking him out of anything. We simply had to decide which of us had the most encouraging silence to go back to.

Encouraging silences fall into a number of interesting categories and are clearly most valuable when they reinforce a negative.

If you happened to be on outpost duty at daylight, one frosty morning in December 1944, near Bastogne, and you did not hear tank engines warming up on the German side of the line, you heard an encouraging silence.

If you have ever thrown a stone into the mouth of a cave that had a multitude of fresh mountain-lion tracks around the entrance, and there was no answering growl, that was an encouraging silence.

If you have ever had a turkey go to roost within 100 yards, and after waiting until nearly dark to slip out and leave, you heard nothing from the roost tree behind you as you tiptoed off, that was an encouraging silence. In every one of these examples, the less you hear the better off you are.

Encouraging silences on the other end of the scale are far more nebulous and subjective.

Precisely what arrangements of the molecules in the air cause you to think a lack of turkey noises in one place is a more encouraging sign than a lack of turkey noises in another place?

I cannot answer the question, but I have come repeatedly to exactly that conclusion.

What form of extrasensory perception can cause you to feel better about returning to one place than another, when you have discovered no fresh evidence of the presence of turkeys in either place? I cannot answer that one either, but I have had those very perceptions.

Because I am perfectly willing to practice five-cent psychiatry without a license, I believe it to be founded in my hatred of ties. I despise them and would rather lose. We came here tied.

I am constitutionally incapable of saying that it doesn't

matter, that one place is about as good as another, that all things are equal. Something in my head, some quirk of character always leads me to a preference. Some piece of data, no matter how thin and ephemeral, causes me to make a choice.

Of course, it can be wrong.

If I have a gift, it is the ability to be wrong in such a sincere tone that other people believe it, and worse, frequently act on the erroneous conclusion.

So the morning of the 29th of April, the second-to-the-last day, the client and I met the sunrise with no single turkey noise intruding to disturb the peace and serenity of the morning. There was not even anything you could exercise your imagination upon.

We stubbornly fought the good fight till 9:00 and came in for breakfast. The school devoted the balance of the morning to an examination of terrain and a session on calling.

The session on calling is always fun for me, and I think, at the end, for the clients, because it consists principally of listening to recordings of real turkeys.

It is almost impossible to explain just how poorly real turkeys call — you have to hear it to believe it — and I sometimes have people ask if the tapes I am using are faked.

They are not. They are absolutely authentic and were recorded by Lovett Williams and David Austin, and the quality of the recording is superb. The quality of the calling is wretched.

If there was such a thing as a live hen decoy, like the calling Susie your great-grandfather used in his duck decoys, and she was tame enough and well trained enough to allow you to enter her in any turkey-calling contest south of Bozeman, Montana, the judges would expel the both of you from the hall.

Not for violating the rules of the contest, because the

callers are out of sight of the judges, but for the quality of the calling.

Very probably, in addition to throwing you out, someone would slash your truck tires in the parking lot as punishment for making a mockery of a serious event.

Real turkeys call so much more poorly than calling contestants that there is no comparison at all.

It is rougher, squeakier, more jerky, too loud, too long. Every fault that can be leveled against a beginning caller can be leveled as easily against a live turkey. Listening to recordings of actual yelping will do more for your confidence than anything else I can think of. In fact, it tends to make you a trifle contemptuous of hens.

The afternoon of the 29th, scouting and hunting alone, was really not hunting. If you find anything in the afternoon, it is obligatory to save it for the morning, as difficult a thing to do as that is. Neither customer nor guest came down here to look at pictures of somebody else's turkey. They expect to be the subject in the picture who is smiling, the one standing next to the subject with his feet tied together on the pole.

I spent most of the afternoon popping up to the infield and dedicatedly running out every pop fly.

I visited every green patch on the 1,000 acres. Moved up to it, after yelping, an inch at a time. This late in the year, and as early as our spring was last year, the ryegrass planted in the green patches was at least waist high, had dried to a pale green, and there were green patches tall enough to hide a turkey even if he were standing in the middle of it.

I looked for tracks and droppings and strut marks, and stopped and yelped from time to time, staying in place for a half-hour in a couple of likely looking spots. I had left the truck in one location and had walked around the perimeter on the road net, working my way back to an area between two large green patches with a pond between them, where I expected to be at flying-up time.

There is a place in there where the gravel road crosses a bridge over a creek with 6-foot banks, makes an abrupt left-hand, right-angle turn just after it crosses the bridge, and then, in another 50 yards, makes an equally abrupt right-hand, right-angle turn. After the left-hand turn, the road runs along the side of one of the overmature ryegrass patches. When it turns back right, it runs along the top of the same green patch for over 150 yards. As you go along the road there, working your way east, there is green patch on your right and woods on your left almost from the time you cross the creek.

I was within 5 yards of the bridge, just about at the point where I could look down into the water itself, when I heard a turkey drum.

Nobody is really sure what a turkey uses to drum with. There used to be a school of thought that held it was the vibration of the primary flight feathers. Audubon calls it the "pulmonic puff." You can pay your money and take your choice.

I think it comes from the voice box rather than the wings, but I don't know how the turkey does it. I feel it almost as much as I hear it, and I have never been able to hear it beyond 80 yards or so. It is exceptionally difficult for me to course; it seems to come from everywhere.

This was close — so close I was convinced he was in the road across the creek, just around the corner beyond the left-hand turn, walking the road along the side of the green patch and drumming as he went.

The wooden bridge was elevated over the creek on a little bit of a fill, the creek swamp was clean of understory, and there was nothing to hide behind in the road. I stepped out of the track itself, cocked sideways on the side of the fill, got the yelper out, and made a soft series of calls.

The drumming would increase in intensity, then fade away until it died out completely. When I clucked once again, it built back up.

I was convinced he was in the road, was walking the 50 yards between the two right-angle turns, and fading out of hearing when he went around the second turn and started across the top of the green patch. I decided to shut up, let him fade out of hearing one more time, and then cross the creek, go the 50 yards to the second right-hand turn, and poke my head slowly around the bend. I expected to see him then, partway across the top side of the green patch on his leisurely way to the big pond between the two patches where I expected him to roost.

He faded away out of hearing. I gave him a minute or two and got up, eased down to the first turn, and poked my head around. I didn't want to rush around the first turn and find him standing in the road halfway to the second.

There was nothing in the road, there was nothing in hearing, so, thinking I was right, I moved briskly down the road toward the second turn.

About halfway there, from the waist-high ryegrass on the right of the road and close enough to touch with a fishing pole, Athos, Porthos, and D'Artagnan came up out of the grass in a simultaneous covey rise and fanned out across the green patch.

Any surprise covey of quail is nerve shattering. Over 50 pounds of turkey gobbler, completely unexpected and at a range of 10 feet, is positively traumatic. An 18-pound turkey can get off the ground quickly, but he has a lot of weight to get in motion, and three of them at once is not so much a flush as it is an explosion. It truly scares you.

I have found over the years that in situations like this, a strange thing happens: For the parts of seconds that it takes to go on, things move into slow motion. I am not so much doing it as I am standing off to the side watching it; and while I can't speed anything up, I don't have to. It is all happening at a comfortable speed.

I remember thinking it was all right to shoot. There were three of them — all monsters — and since I had already startled them, the sound of a shot would not make a particle of difference when we came back in the morning.

They had very nearly let me walk right by. Another two or three steps, and I would have been past them; because when they got up, they were distinctly behind my right shoulder.

I shot Athos, the left-hand musketeer, dead in the air at 30 yards, and he hit the ground in the middle of the green patch with a solid thump you could have heard for 100 yards. The whole thing is printed on my retina and will be there till the boneyard.

Athos, with his wings folded, against the line of trees at the other end of the patch, with the other two still gaining altitude as they came up to full speed.

Totally inartistic, totally unearned, not called up in a game of woodland chess and shot neatly in the head, but kicked up out of the grass and shot in the ass at 30 yards, with no more respect for his dignity than if he had been a quail.

I cannot imagine what happened. There was absolutely no eye contact. I was concentrating on the next turn in the road and moving to get there as quickly as I could with the intention of getting down on at least one knee before peeking around the corner at the long straight stretch across the top of the patch. They were in a piece of terrain I had closed out of my consciousness, and if they had waited another second and a half, I would have been by and gone.

Turkeys may operate in flocks, but a flock is simply a collection of individuals, it is not the same mindless entity that inhabited a flock of passenger pigeons.

Somebody lost his nerve, panicked, and flushed. Once

one started, the other two had to go along. If there is any justice in the world, the guilty party should have been Athos because Athos is the one that paid for the mistake.

It makes you wonder how many times nobody panics. How often, and over how many days, do you walk that close to one or more turkeys that do not lose their nerve, know you are not aware of their presence, and simply sit there until you are gone.

It points out something else, too: Things always even out.

The season ended for me the last day before the school started. It is unrealistic for me to expect to kill a turkey during the school. In the morning I am with a client, and in the afternoon I am trying to find a candidate for a client to work with the next day. To expect to find multiple candidates in the afternoon, in a situation that would not affect the next morning adversely, is the equivalent of asking for the moon.

But the percentages are inexorable.

Last season I earned two turkeys. The turkeys I called into the road in central Florida on the second day of the season, and the turkey I called up and let go the afternoon of April 19.

Last season I killed two turkeys.

The fact that the ones I shot were the breadth of the season apart and did not happen to be the ones I earned is immaterial. The percentages do not say when it will happen. They guarantee only that sooner or later, it will occur.

It is the reason why the statue of Justice, holding the scales, is always depicted blindfolded.

15

FINALE

The final morning, Sunday, April 30th, closed the season with the same kind of plain-vanilla performance as the first day had begun it.

If either Porthos or D'Artagnan gobbled, neither of us heard them, although we were in the proper location between the two ponds at the proper time. I knew where they had flown the night before, and I knew there had not been enough daylight after the covey rise for them to have relaxed, come down out of the trees, and walked off very far. They had to be in hearing range, which didn't mean that either of them had to gobble.

A turkey did gobble, away down southeast of us, and there was a gravel road going in that direction. We started to him almost at a trot. He gobbled once more while we were on the way and then either he — or another turkey — gobbled on the ground behind us after we got as close as we dared go. I was not at all sure it was the same one, but it was a turkey, we were reasonably close to something, and it was worth playing the hand as dealt for whatever it was.

It turned out to be not much of a hand, and it didn't get any better after the draw either, because we never heard another sound. I was afraid to do any amount of prowling because we did have a little something to work with. There was no use trying to locate something already on the ground, with hens, for tomorrow. In the first place, any hen that was not totally maladjusted had been in the incubation phase of nesting for two weeks. In the second, there was not going to be any tomorrow.

So we sat, and yelped, and gobbled, and imitated gobbler fights and did all the forlorn things you do right there at the last, simply to show which side you are on. We finally gave up and took the last walk back.

The last walk back, on the last day, is not simply a return to the vehicle to go home. It is more of a walk down memory lane than it is anything else.

As a general rule, I do it alone. Normally I feel it is as important to go alone the last day as it is the first, and this last year is one of the few times I have been with anyone else at the end.

I usually finish at the magic corner, where twenty years ago the Colonel's daughter watched me strangle the turkey to death, hand to hand, in thigh-deep water. Unless the season has been particularly unsuccessful, I unload the gun when I get up to start walking. I unload on the theory that the season is over, the trip back to the car is a trip through limbo, and any turkey stumbled over at that time ought to be home free because he belongs to next year.

The client commented on my total change in demeanor. He had heard me say more than once during the school that you will have substantially more success if you can conduct yourself as if there were a turkey within 100 yards, every minute you are in the woods. He said I acted as if we were behind 40-to-nothing and were in the final two minutes of play. Of course, he was right.

The walk back is a contemplative walk mostly, and a totally relaxed one always, because you are no longer hunting. You are looking back across the entire continuum and filing the entire season away in your mind. This is only the beginning of the harvest. The total harvest generally takes a couple of weeks. Sometimes, weeks after that, some pungent memory comes to the surface that needs to be added to the collection.

Which is all as it should be.

We have those sharp-pointed canines and have our eyes in the front of our heads because we are hunters and predators. The prey have their eyes on the sides, to enable them to look out for us. Our weak and flimsy fingernails and toenails are the last vestiges of claws.

As we have evolved, we have had to make adjustments. None of us could make it very long if we were forced to live naked in the woods and use our predatory eyes and fangs and claws to run down food, tear it to shreds with our talons, rip it from the bone with our fangs, and eat it raw.

We order pizza on the telephone or go to the kitchen and make bologna sandwiches instead.

And in addition to the loss of these physical abilities, we have lost a large part of our primitive instincts. They may have been present at birth, but through disuse and neglect have become as weak and insufficient as our vestigial fangs and talons.

In one sense, it is an advantage.

A wild creature can never afford to relax. He must remain cocked and loaded all the time because, if he does not, one of two things can happen. Either he misses something to eat, or something bigger eats him for lunch. His instincts keep him in battery all the time. Rarely, if ever, can he afford to let up.

He can sleep, but he cannot contemplate.

We, on the other hand, although it may take some time to work ourselves into the pitch of the season, can take an even longer time to work our way back down. Because, coming down, there is no calendar and there are no instincts to keep the strings tight.

We are able, at leisure, to take an incident at a time, a scene at time, a day at a time, and call it back, and brush it off and look at it, and polish it up and refile it to be reexamined later, if we choose.

That is why the after-season personal-critique stage can be even more enjoyable than the anticipation stage, unless you happen to be one of those empty-headed optimists who thinks nothing should ever go wrong. In that case, the critique stage of every season you live through will be unsatisfactory.

I have had way more seasons than my share, way more than I ever expected to have, but hopefully have several more to come.

Every one of them has been more thorn than rose, but every one of them has been marked by singularly bright roses and singularly dull thorns. In one respect, I may be the most fortunate of men. The roses are no brighter and the thorns no duller in the older memories than they are in the recent.

The good old days are right this minute.

Sicut erat in principio, et nunc, et semper.